Lessons in
Elemental Style

by Steven Calantropio

A collection of works in elemental style with detailed process teaching notes
and suggestions for further development and improvisation

SMC 582

SCHOTT

Mainz • London • Madrid • New York • Paris • Prague • Tokyo • Toronto

This book is dedicated to Adele Castaldo,
my life companion, lover and friend
who is always there for me.

SMC 582

ISMN M–60001–232–9
UPC   841886025950
ISBN   978–1–84761–404–9

Design, typesetting and music engraving by William Holab

Contents

Acknowledgements

It is a relatively easy task to create a meaningful and enjoyable career in music education. The very nature of collaborative artistic experiences will bind you and your students in a way unlike any other area of study. Work hard, stay interested and involved in your profession and the people around you. Seek out and learn from fine mentors, regardless of their age. Rejoice in your students' achievements and learn from your own mistakes. Do not get overly involved with the political winds that blow one way this year and another the following. You will be rewarded with a lifetime of stimulating aesthetic experiences and the thanks of the many souls for whom you have provided a candle to light the way.

I acknowledge those individuals who by their sheer commitment to music and education mentored me both actively and passively: Jane Frazee, Brigitte Warner, Richard Gill, Lawrence Wheeler and Barbara Haselbach first come to mind although many hands and minds have shaped my own.

Thanks to those teachers, students and colleagues both young and old who have surrounded me over the years and made me become a better teacher. Donna Fleetwood, Matt McCoy, Arvida Steen, Valerie Peters, Linda O'Donnell, Cyndee Giebler, Jay Broeker, Catherine West and Robyn Stavely along with the members of the Orff Institute Special Class of 1981–82; brothers and sisters in music and movement whose friendships have sustained me in good and bad times and always challenged me to do better.

I am indebted to Wendy Lampa of Schott publishers who encourages me through her willingness to publish my books.

Of course, I am most grateful to my life partner of many years, Adele Castaldo who patiently edits my work, listens to my complaints, answers my questions and gives me the time and space to consider my work carefully.

—STEVEN CALANTROPIO
MARCH 2015

Part 1

About This Book

Lessons in Elemental Style is the author's second collection of original works and folk music arrangements with detailed process teaching steps and suggestions. The first collection, *Pieces and Processes* (SMC #569) has been accepted as a standard text in the study of Orff-Schulwerk teaching process. *Lessons in Elemental Style* is both a continuation and elaboration of the ideas and materials found in the earlier book.

Both of these texts have come to publication after much analysis of my pedagogical work with both adults and children. On the one hand, I believe it is the responsibility of any dedicated music teacher to move beyond the 'recipe' style lesson found in many publications and music series texts. When teachers take the step of discovering, arranging or composing new materials for their students, they transcend to a higher level of commitment to their students' aesthetic growth as well as to their own. The instructor's efforts can be interpreted as the growth from apprentice to journeyman; a move towards increased competency and professionalism which should be encouraged and celebrated.

Such personal growth is often tentative and halting as the teacher initially struggles to create his or her own new lesson materials modeled after the lessons of others that have been successful in the past. All teachers need effective models to serve as points of reference when they hit the inevitable stumbling blocks on the way to instructional self-sufficiency. The need for detailed, step-by-step process lessons is greatest at the moment when no ideas come; when the music teacher 'hits the pedagogical wall'; when the desire to be original and creative faces the frightening momentary void of inspiration for the next step.

This book was compiled with the purpose of creating a thoroughly-processed set of lessons directed towards the development of musical skills and concepts. The lesson's purpose is to provide tools to work through the sticking points that music teachers inevitably experience at some juncture as they stretch and grow. Each of the lessons should be viewed as both a reproducible model for upper grade elementary school students experienced in elemental music-making and also as a collection of ideas, processes, sources and improvisational concepts that can be adapted and used as tools in developing other experiences.

The lessons contained in this edition span a stylistic range from the most traditional of folk-songs arranged in parts to experimental ideas that mirror contemporary trends in music. While no collection can fill every need, *Lessons in Elemental Style* seeks to provide some of the tools music educators need to effectively teach lessons of their own design as they assimilate the important skills of process teaching and lesson development that are presented here.

What is Elemental Style

For years music educators have struggled to come up with a clear, succinct answer when asked "what is elemental style?" For the most part, they have been unsuccessful. Defining a musical style is not an easy task. While we may think that we have a clear definition in mind, when pressed we find that our definition is not as comprehensive as we thought it to be. Rather than defining a style, musicians often define eras of western music in terms of chronological periods; for example, the Romantic period, the Baroque period, etc. As one style develops into another, we are actually looking at a segment of a continuum of musical development and practice. Stylistic identifiers come in and out of favor; sometimes slowly as a musical idiom reaches the end of its creative possibilities or sometimes quickly as when social, economic or political influences demand change.

Elemental style is particularly difficult to define. One reason is that there has always been elemental music. Since the earliest times, the primal human urge to create music and associate it with movement and dance often involving the entire social group has been part of the human experience. The songs, dances, chants and rituals of primeval times are passed along through the oral tradition of tribes, cultures, societies and religions and are not dependent upon written notation. They often employ the simplest of musical media; the ability to sing and move to the singing, the clapping of hands or striking of other body parts with the hands, the stamping of feet, the repeated chanting or playing of a short pattern gaining power through many repetitions, the use of an unmoving single note accompaniment to thicken the musical texture.

Elemental music draws upon these primal musical expressions to create a style which is integral to the culture whence it comes. This foundation of cultural materials is not related to the developments of a culture's art music although there are often common elements in both.

The modern emphasis on elemental style began with Carl Orff (1895–1982) and his collaborator Gunild Keetman (1904–1990) who combined these primal musical expressions into their experiments with young dancer/musicians beginning in the 1920s. Orff began to refer to the music created by dancers, who also played percussion to accompany their movement as elemental. It focused on the primary components of music in their purest and simplest expressions. His continued work with Keetman through the years of World War II and into the next two decades became known as Schulwerk, literally "school work" but probably better understood as "a schooling in music and dance." Orff and Keetman's publications were published under the Schulwerk masthead and it became clear that they had overseen the reincarnation of the ancient beginnings of elemental music.

Careful study of the Orff/Keetman Schulwerk materials provides a set of stylistic descriptors of elemental music that can help individuals understand what is intended by the use of the term elemental style. A musical style is determined by a loose set of artistic boundaries that govern what does and what doesn't fit. If we can identify elemental music, we can then identify elemental style as the modes of expression that employ elemental music. Orff and Keetman's adaptations of the previously discussed primal expressive musical impulses used in their Schulwerk materials provides us with the following identifiers of elemental style.

- Elemental music and elemental style are not intellectually based but draw upon the natural urges of human beings to express themselves. The most natural means of expression occurs in the actions that we do most of the time; we speak and we move. The use of speech and movement is fundamental to elemental style. Speech eventually leads to song; movement leads to dance. These developments require no significant intellectual preparation but occur naturally. Because of this, we consider elemental music as being "near the earth" to paraphrase Orff from one of his talks on the subject.

- Elemental music is pattern based. Short repeated patterns of speech, movement, rhythm, harmony, melody and form are used to develop musical ideas. As repetition represents the simplest way of developing music, it is fundamental to the style. The repetition of short patterns create the accompaniment styles of elemental music and are termed ostinati. The use of ostinato patterns is one of the hallmarks of elemental style.

- While some musical styles seek to expand upon previous developments and extensions of musical components, elemental style consciously limits such developments. Therefore, the simplest uses of musical tools are favored over the more complex ones. Melodic material begins with two note chants, three note calls, pentatonic idioms and traditional diatonic modalities. Chromaticism is not part of this system nor is modulation, harmonic schemes other than drones or simple major and minor triads nor any ambiguities caused by the use of diminished or augmented intervals or triads. Clarity is the goal of elemental style and ambiguity is shunned for the sake of a straightforward and understandable syntax of musical elements.

- Elemental music is easily broken down into its component elements. Rhythm can be isolated from melody, harmonic progressions are easily discernible from the melodies they accompany, canonic episodes are easily seen first as unison patterns. Because of this, elemental music in our time exists primarily for pedagogical purposes. The ability to simplify music by isolating and exploring its different component elements allows students to assimilate each component before seeing it in conjunction with other elements.

- Elemental music employs instruments that are easily accessible and require little training or technique to play. For the most part, the unpitched percussion and barred pitched percussion instruments used in elemental music draw upon the human body's large muscle groups and because of this, such instruments are immediately accessible to children who often lack the fine motor skills necessary for more sophisticated and advanced instrumental performance.

- Those who approach elemental music do so on the basis of the desire to create music quickly. Because of the pattern based nature of elemental style, it is most often learned through rote repetition and memorization. Complex note reading skills are not required although such skills, when used on a limited basis, can enhance the teaching/learning process. While varied learning styles are part of any fine teaching and learning, the visual emphasis on note reading is bypassed by the ability to hear and memorize musical patterns of rhythm, melody, harmony, form, etc. The desire for a more immediate basis for musical expression other than traditional composition leads to the use of improvisation which is encouraged in all elemental media (speech, singing, movement, percussion, recorder) at various points in the teaching process. Improvisation can be considered as a form of musical extension which develops either spontaneously or from a previously composed work. It can also be used as an assessment tool for conceptual learning in a pedagogical setting.

Distilling the content of the previous six paragraphs, here is the author's best attempt to define elemental music briefly and concisely. Elemental music:

- is based on speech and movement
- is primarily rhythmic in nature
- is pattern based in rhythm, melody, harmony, form
- is memorized after being taught by rote with little or no use of musical notation
- is auditory based rather than visually based
- employs instruments that require unsophisticated playing technique (outside of the recorder) and with limited timbral colors
- stimulates improvisation in all media
- uses a limited melodic and harmonic vocabulary
- is primarily pedagogically based.

In creating *Lessons in Elemental Style* it is the author's goal to provide the reader with an intermediate to advanced collection of varied experiences drawing upon the concepts suggested in the previous paragraphs. Movement and improvisation are encouraged in every experience. Each lesson begins with a simple idea which is then developed through process teaching techniques into a larger form. Traditional melodies are balanced by composed works; experimental concepts are balanced by traditional orchestrations. Each lesson offers suggestions for divergent development based on ideas, skills or concepts found in the lesson flow. Each experience will help both teacher and student further define elemental music and style by affirming the natural, organic music-making possibilities inherent in all.

Lesson Flow and Structure

The structure of an elemental music lesson should be well-planned long in advance of the actual lesson presentation. In organizing the components of such a lesson, one needs to consider what I have called lesson flow. Lesson flow is the overriding sense of logical movement from one episode of the lesson to the next. A smooth lesson flow will captivate students' curiosity from the start and keep them engaged through the lesson development. It allows students to feel successful in the artistic tasks assigned to them while providing the teacher with opportunities to assess student learning. A concept or skill-based lesson with a well-organized lesson flow becomes a standard in the teacher's pedagogical collection, to be used time and time again. Such lessons should be subject to review and with such review, they can be elaborated or revised, extended or shortened, isolated or connected with other experiences.

An effective lesson flow depends on two criteria being met. First, the many small sequential steps of lesson development should be consciously placed to create a lesson process which is often referred to as being 'spiral' in nature. Moving from a seminal initial idea, new material is developed around and moving away from the starting point, building on what is already known and has been experienced. As a lesson process is taking place, the cognitive movement from the center of the spiral outward is almost imperceptible to the students because each step is integrated with what came before and leads to what follows. Consider the diagram (below) which shows the first 20 steps in the spiral development of Lesson # 3 *To Work Upon the Railway*. A fine teacher, whose consciousness is attuned to process teaching, might discern even smaller pedgogical increments between some of the 20 steps in the graphic.

The need for such additional steps will be dependent upon the teacher's perceived success of students and their readiness to move forward in the process. The goal is to provide a smooth, seamless lesson "roadway" without any sudden bumps or potholes created by steps that are too far away from each other in skill development or cognitive understanding.

Teaching Models

Convergent Lesson Focus

Another consideration in developing an effective process lesson is that of lesson focus. When considering lesson focus, we look at the larger philosophical direction in play as a lesson moves from introductory explorations to the refinement of a finished work and continuing on to improvisational experiences

We can group lesson focus into two specific models which I will call the Convergent model and the Divergent model. In the Convergent model, the process begins with playful but well-guided exploration by students who have no specific end point in mind. These introductory steps might include review of an earlier lesson, a singing game or play party, a passing game, an elimination game, an improvisational strategy, a rhythmic echo experience or any such activity that begins to bring students' attention to the musical materials that will be part of the completed lesson. With a predetermined end point always in mind, the instructor directs students through a set of responses that will lead to the assimilation of the chosen example. Teaching of melody and melodic structure, accompaniment patterns, ostinati, orchestration and form all lead students to the eventual learning of a predetermined example which might be a selection from the Orff-Schulwerk volumes, an orchestrated folk-song, a creative movement episode, a recorder piece or work for mallet instruments, a rhythmic piece for unpitched instruments or body percussion, etc. The idea of convergent lesson focus is to lead from many seemingly unstructured starting points to the learning of a well-defined musical example. This process might best be illustrated graphically, thus:

Convergent Lesson Development
Convergent development moves from many open-ended exploratory ideas to the specific ideas required for the development of a pre-chosen example.

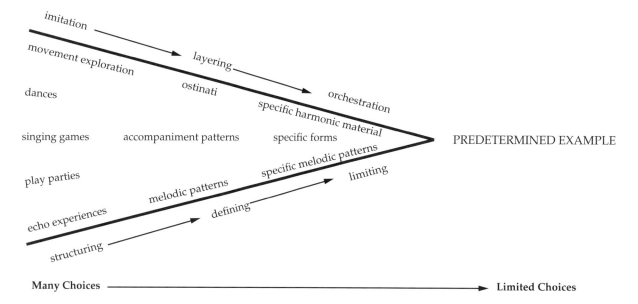

Divergent Lesson Focus

Divergent teaching focus follows the reverse flow of the convergent model. Divergent teaching begins with a simple musical element: a rhythm, a metric pattern, a scale, a gesture or series of steps, a mode or sequence of pitches, etc. This element serves as the starting point for lesson development in which the initial seed idea is expanded through manipulation and development. Repetition, being the most primary form of musical development, is used extensively in this process. Other developmental procedures are also employed: variations of the original idea, introduction of complementary or contrasting ideas, development of accompaniment, instrumentation, improvisation, the addition of movement, etc. Unlike the convergent model, no clear or predetermined ending point is imagined at the outset of the lesson by either teacher or student. The lesson culminates when the developmental process reaches a point of musical satisfaction for all involved. We can graph the divergent model as illustrated:

Divergent Lesson Development
Divergent development moves from a specific musical idea through developmental processes towards an open-ended conclusion that is not predetermined by teacher or student.

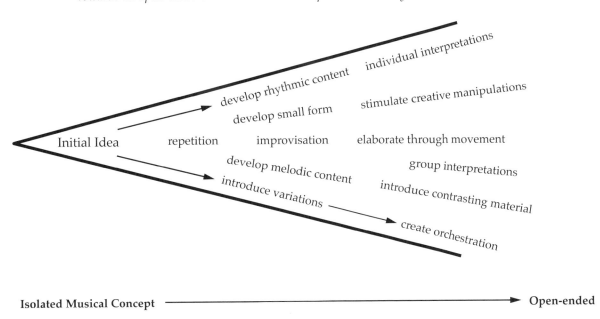

One can easily see that the two models move in opposite philosophical directions. The intuitive educator will understand that there are both positive and negative aspects to each lesson focus model.

Pros and Cons

Convergent teaching is best suited to the introduction, development and assimilation of specific sequential musical skills and concepts that are organized in a curricular framework. Rooted in accountability, it is a process that provides an answer to the question "what was taught/learned in this lesson?". The growing prevalence of learning standards and benchmarks on a national, state and even local level is best handled through convergent lessons that address a specific skill or concept. However, such convergent lesson focus when overly strict, tends to limit student input and creativity by working towards predetermined end points which, while musically satisfying as artistic models, can be reached only through the limitation of student experimentation and choice. In the final analysis, there is limited opportunity for student input of ideas in a convergent experience as the predetermined example dictates what must be learned.

Divergent teaching, on the other hand, addresses and compels creative student input by the very lack of a predetermined endpoint. It is almost exclusively improvisational in nature as new creations spring from careful consideration of ideas being generated. Student suggestions are openly solicited, tried out and either accepted or rejected by the group. The teacher acts as a facilitator in such a process, making sure that all student input is considered and fairly evaluated while also inserting a suggestion or idea when student creativity begins to falter. Divergent lessons may follow completely different developmental paths than what might have been imagined by the instructor at the outset of the experiences and the final results may be quite unanticipated. As divergent experiences are built upon student input, they readily take ownership of such experiences and, as a result, feel affinity towards their efforts both as individuals and as a group. The downside of the divergent process is that such experiences are often very time consuming; ample "think time" must be allowed for and the trying out of numerous ideas and solutions can consume much class time. Such lessons sometimes tend to "wander" as new ideas are tried out and accepted or rejected. The final result may not focus on any specific musical skill or concept other than the creation of an artistic product, surely a worthwhile goal in aesthetic education, but one not necessarily associated with a particular skill or concept that needs to be addressed at that point in a curricular framework. In addition, the ability to teach exclusively from a standpoint of improvisation and open-ended creativity is a pedagogical skill that very few have acquired. In my many years of working with well-meaning, dedicated music teachers, I have found few who can do this. It seems that for the most part, we are just not trained and encouraged to think and perform in this manner.

The apparent oppositions of Convergent and Divergent lesson focus puts music educators in a quandary. On the one hand, we are encouraged to approach the learning of musical skills and concepts in a well-organized, curricular manner presenting sequential skills, developing them while assessing their assimilation before moving ahead. On the other hand, we are taught to value and actively solicit student input in lessons, to instill a sense of ownership by students in their work and to allow for open-ended creativity in its most exciting and expressive possibilities.

The nature of elemental music suggests a solution to this predicament. Elemental music is by nature flexible, malleable and able to be explored through its component parts. The elements of rhythm, melody, harmony and form can be readily studied in isolation from each other. I would propose a third lesson flow model that combines both the convergent and divergent elements previously discussed. In this model, which we will call the Elemental Model, a predetermined musical work is identified and taught using the convergent process. If a chosen example is truly elemental in nature, it will lend itself to variation and manipulation right from the very start. As the example is learned, distinct musical skills or concepts relating to sequential curricular steps can be identified. Once the musical example is learned, a relevant curricular skill or concept is isolated and becomes the starting point for the divergent process. Ideally, divergent procedures reinforce a specific skill or concept while soliciting creative student input. The overriding energy in such a two-part lesson is drawn from improvisation which can occur at multiple loci through both sides of the process but is particularly important at the point where the convergent and divergent models meet. In the Elemental Model, curricular goals can be addressed, student input and creativity can be solicited through different learning modalities while lessons efficiently use the limited time given to music classes.

The Elemental Model

...allows for the addressing of specific curricular skills, the efficient learning of a high quality model and the solicitation of creative student input through improvisatory experiences.

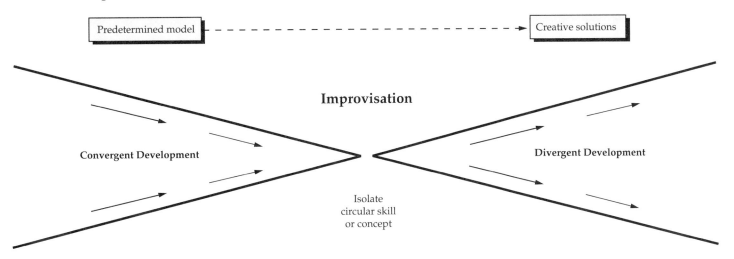

At this point, it should be evident that the key to the development of successful lessons using the Elemental Model is choosing an appropriate example that is musically malleable and displays the clear use of one or more musical elements, skills or concepts. The works of Carl Orff and Gunild Keetman in the *Music for Children* series, also known as the Orff-Schulwerk present hundreds of such example pieces. While not every piece in the *Music for Children* series lends itself to successful lesson development, the collection provides a wealth of stimulating material to fill the needs of music teachers, particularly when supplemented with folk-song arrangements, original teacher and student composed works and selections from the art music repertoire that display clearly identifiable musical ideas.

Lessons in Elemental Style provides the reader with suggestions for divergent exercises for each exercise whenever divergent development is appropriate. The divergent flow of these lessons should be, by nature, more representative of the individual teacher and student's creative ideas rather than the author's. Hence this part of each lesson is left intentionally undeveloped so that the individual inclinations of the teacher and his or her students can take their own course.

How to Use this Book

Lessons in Elemental Style has been written with a two-fold purpose:

1. First, to provide Orff-Schulwerk teachers and others interested in elemental style with a collection of intermediate lessons for students with significant experiences in elemental music learning. These lessons are therefore intended for upper grade elementary schools, middle school or secondary school music classrooms or as model lessons for those studying for a career in music education.

2. Secondly, the lessons are created to provide detailed lesson process used to develop and explore intermediate elemental materials. It is the author's opinion that the majority of elemental music publications are directed towards early primary school students. These lessons provide teaching processes for more involved concepts of melody, harmony, rhythm, form, etc.

In using this book, success will be dependent upon the students' ability to hear, remember, understand, imitate and manipulate patterns of melody, rhythm, harmony and form. Students must be willing and able to sing in tune and move unselfconsciously. They must also have experience in instrument playing, particularly unpitched and barred percussion instruments. Without significant experience in elemental music learning styles, both pupil and teacher will struggle with the materials presented here. However, if students are well-prepared with many experiences in elemental music, are adventurous and fairly skilled in the elemental media (speech, singing, movement, body percussion, unpitched percussion, barred instruments and recorder) they will find this collection a stimulating and rewarding set of experiences that opens the doors to further creation and development of both group and individual ideas.

Using these materials requires significant preparation by the instructor. I suggest that only one lesson be attempted at a time during a teacher's busy weekly schedule. Most of the lessons will require more than one typical (40–45 minute) music class, particularly when exploring the divergent ideas given towards the end of each lesson. Teachers should read the lesson repeatedly, trying out and becoming familiar with the developmental steps of the lesson process. In a spirit of joyful cooperative exploration, the teacher should present the materials carefully, always striving for musicality and accuracy but remaining open to student responses outside of those that are expected. Teachers may discover that there are intermediate process steps that can be taken to develop the lesson that are not included here and should feel free to insert these steps into the lesson process when necessary.

Any of the lessons presented here may result in a performance piece which can be presented either formally or informally. When students feel that they truly know the composition, they are always willing to share it. Sharing musical accomplishments with others is one reason we maintain the performing arts. The communication established between performers and listeners is key to the individual's perceptions of the importance of what they are doing.

As with most lessons, there can be multiple stopping points where a sense of completion can terminate the lesson experience. Equally, teachers should not be bound by the limits of the printed page but should feel free to continue exploring the direction which the lesson has taken. It is the journey (lesson process) as well as the destination (final 'performance') that are equally as important in elemental style.

A very important point must be made here. Elemental music teaching requires a high level of commitment by the instructor. The teaching processes presented for each lesson are provided to show how materials can be broken down into their smallest component parts and presented in a sequential manner that follows the spiral-shaped developmental process presented earlier. While there is great value in initially replicating a lesson step-by-step as it is presented in a written text, the whole goal of *Lessons in Elemental Style* is to stimulate readers to develop their own lesson processes and materials. The adaptation of the teaching process steps, exploratory techniques and developmental ideas in this book is of paramount importance. "Recipe" style textbooks such as this one should only serve to stimulate new ideas and thinking once a lesson has been replicated. *It is not the intention of the author simply to provide all of the steps of any particular lesson but rather to stimulate creative educators to teach their own materials using their own variations and adaptations of the processes and materials presented here.*

The Role of Improvisation in Lessons in Elemental Style

At many points in this book, teachers are encouraged to explore basic lesson concepts through improvisation. The importance of improvisation as lessons move from convergent flow to divergent development cannot be overestimated. As well as providing students with a sense of ownership of concepts and materials, improvisation is an assessment tool that gives insight into the student's level of understanding and competency. Improvisational episodes in well-structured lessons can provide some of the most stimulating moments in an individual's musical growth.

It is not the purpose of this book to serve as a primer in the art of improvisation. The subject of improvisation in an educational setting needs to be addressed in a comprehensive overview that would systematically approach both the creative and utilitarian aspects of the skill. While the world of music educators still awaits such a thorough study, *Lessons in Elemental Style* can help to provide some basic templates for student improvisation.

Highly valued in many historical periods and social contexts, musical improvisation finds its greatest exponents today in the worlds of pop music and jazz. Outside of these two genres, we find improvisation alive among current 'new age' artists, as part of many ethnic and world music styles and somewhat among church organists where this skill has been a requisite for centuries. Music educators have only recently begun to recognize the value of improvisation in pedagogical work. It is not surprising that most traditionally trained music educators have little or no experience in improvisation either as teachers or as performers. While many of the underlying skills needed to improvise in popular music, jazz and new age styles are the same as those we expect our music students to assimilate, the study of these genres is beyond the scope of this book. *Lessons in Elemental Style* focuses on improvisation for pedagogical purposes in an education setting.

The art of improvisation can be described as the creation of music while it is being performed. Though on the surface such experiences seem to be spontaneous, the fact is that the artist, either consciously or unconsciously, accesses both an internal vocabulary of ideas (scales, chords, rhythms, harmonic patterns, forms, etc.) and a syntax with which to present them. Vocabulary and syntax are internalized from significant experiences in music, making the case for considerable study and exploration of a defined musical model or style before an improvisation should begin. Rather than leaving the performer alone to structure all aspects of an improvisational episode, the improviser is best served when most of the musical elements of an improvisation are structured in advance leaving only one or two parameters open for creative solutions. Lessons in improvisation therefore must not be improvised but should be thoroughly structured and carefully planned for student success.

The following is an improvisation toolbox offered to help the reader organize his or her work in improvisation with children. It is a collection of tools that are organized around specific musical elements such as those that bridge the convergent and divergent connecting point of the Elemental Model discussed above. Successful improvisation will depend on many factors: student experience and preparation, facility with musical materials and media and a non-judgmental environment where risk taking is encouraged and celebrated.

A Toolbox for Improvisation

Rhythmic Improvisation

- At first, limit rhythmic improvisation to the rhythmic elements found in the example. Identify rhythmic elements in the model both visually and aurally. Encourage the simple manipulation of the elements into different patterns and organizations.
- Ask students to transpose a rhythm in simple meter (2/4, 3/4, 4/4, etc.) into compound meter (3/8, 6/8, etc.) or into irregular meter (5/4, 7/8, etc.).
- Challenge students to employ a distinctive rhythmic pattern a predetermined number of times in the improvisation (for example, "use four sixteenth notes only once in your improvisation," "use it twice," etc.).
- Ask students to consciously use repetition in their creation.
- Require students to employ timed silence (rest) in their creations.
- Use Question/Answer strategies between two performers. Once secure, ask individuals to provide both question and answer.
- Improvise in pairs, trios or small groups. Remind participants to listen closely to the texture they are creating and avoid too much sound at one time or by any one player. Encourage the use of silence as part of the improvisation. Discuss the timbre and sustained qualities of each instrument and how those specific qualities can work with the rest of the group.

Melodic Improvisation

- Give starting and ending pitches for the improvised melody.
- Provide a graphic image for students to follow showing various melodic curves (ascending, descending, alternating high-low, smooth, angular, etc.). Eliminate part of the curve and ask them to create a new one.
- Discuss the concept of steps, skips and repetitions of pitches pointing out that the primary movement of melody is by stepwise motion or a skip of a third.
- Provide a "row" of un-timed pitches (written as whole notes) asking students to follow the row. Allow for repetition of pitches, different note lengths, octave displacements, doubling back in the row, etc. Ask for student interpretations.
- Start with a limited tonal set (for example, three stepwise pitches, pentatonic, etc.) and then allow for other pitches to be added into the improvisation one at a time.
- Discuss the manipulation of a series of pitches through augmentation, diminution, inversion, retrograde.
- Use phrase length characteristics to organize an improvisation: four equal phrases, combination of short or long phrases, etc.
- Use trichords as the basis for melodic improvisation. Trichords are three contiguous scale degrees that move in a stepwise ascending or descending motion. Stringing together multiple trichord patterns can create longer melodic phrases. The last pitch of one trichord (1), one step above it (2) or below it (3) serves as the starting pitch of the next unit. Observe the example below in E

Aeolian. At first create the trichord flow without rhythm or meter (example #1). Then develop rhythmic flow and center the melody in a specified meter (example #2).

Harmonic Improvisation

- Improvise melodies in various modes over drone accompaniments discussing which pitches will sound best over such accompaniments. Use rhythmic structures to organize these melodies.
- Employ pentatonic improvisations above stepwise triadic ostinati that are hexatonic or diatonic in nature (e.g., tonic-supertonic, tonic-subtonic).
- When improvising over functional harmonic changes, display triad notation and have students move from one triad member (root, third, fifth) of the first triad to the closest pitch in the next harmony in un-timed rhythm. Use a finger snap or a hand clap to indicate the next triad. Have students begin on different starting points, looking for common tones between two triads. Eventually move from triad to triad rhythmically (see p. 66 "Four Steps to Melodic Improvistation").

Structure and Form

- Ask students to consciously create rhythmic improvisations using the five elemental structures or templates below. Such improvisations intentionally use clearly repeated phrases or semi-phrases as well as contrasting elements to create the structure. Use these structures in conjunction with other suggestions in the previous categories. Once a rhythmic structure has been created, it can easily transfer to melody. Repeated A sections need only be the same rhythm, the actual melodic pitches may change or stay the same.

Part 2

1. Hey, Ho, to the Greenwood

William Byrd
(1543–1623)

Hey, ho_____ to the green - wood now let us go, sing hey___ and

ho. And there shall we find both buck and doe, sing hey___ and ho.

The hart, the hind and the pret-ty lit - tle doe, sing hey___ and ho.

This energetic hunting canon provides teachers with a chance to process-teach a traditional art music canon in their elemental music classes. William Byrd was a master English composer of the late Renaissance whose polyphonic works included canons such as *Hey, Ho, to the Greenwood*. Elemental process-teaching techniques work well with many selected art-music examples. While most American children are aware that male and female white-tailed deer are named "buck" and "doe" respectively, they may not be aware of a smaller species of deer, common in Europe, called the Roe-deer whose gender names are "hart" (male) and "hind" (female).

EXPLORATION

1. Process-teaching often begins with finding repeated patterns within the music that can become starting points. The musical phrase " sing hey, and ho" straddles measures 4 and 5, 8 and 9 and 13–15. Prepare this pattern as follows:

Teacher (T.) and Students (S.) sing up and down the C Ionian scale. T. then sings the ascending scale while S. sing the descending scale. T. asks students to sing the descending scale imitating the changes that T. introduces in the ascending pattern:

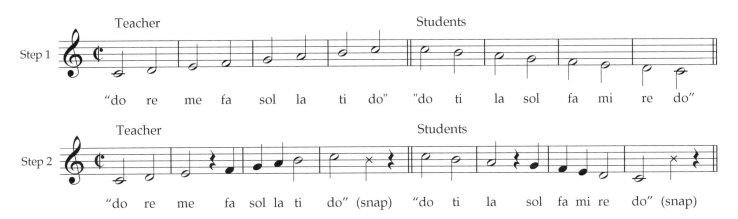

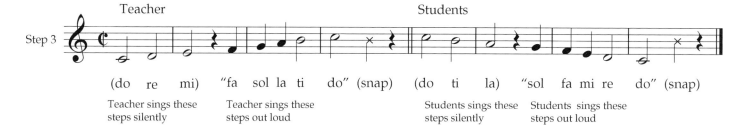

Step 3

(do re mi) "fa sol la ti do" (snap)   (do ti la) "sol fa mi re do" (snap)

Teacher sings these   Teacher sings these   Students sings these   Students sings these
steps silently   steps out loud   steps silently   steps out loud

Once students have isolated the melodic pattern "sol-fa-mi-re-do," have them sing the pattern using the song text "...sing hey and ho":

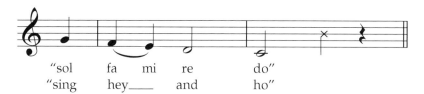

"sol fa mi re do"
"sing hey___ and ho"

2.   T. asks the students to move through space freely around the room, stepping the half-note pulse. The students move 8 steps followed immediately by singing the previously identified pattern. Next try singing the pattern after 5 steps and again after a further 5 steps creating a sequence of 8 steps, 5 steps, 5 steps:

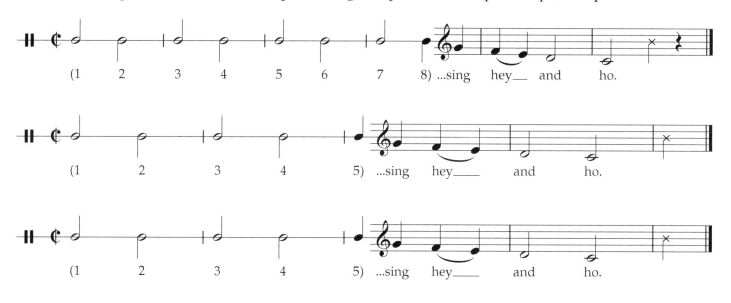

(1   2   3   4   5   6   7   8) ...sing hey___ and ho.

(1   2   3   4   5) ...sing hey___ and ho.

(1   2   3   4   5) ...sing hey___ and ho.

Challenge S. to repeat the same stepping-singing process outlined above, but now T. speaks the remainder of the text while students move. They respond with "sing hey and ho."

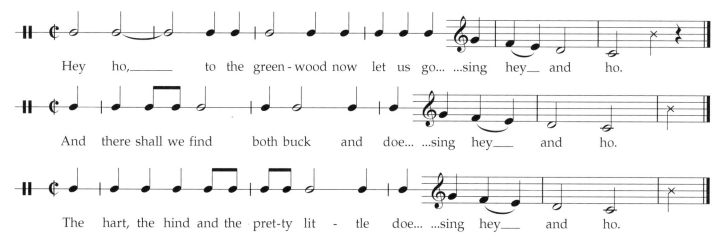

Hey ho,___   to the green-wood now let us go... ...sing hey__ and ho.

And   there shall we find   both buck   and   doe... ...sing hey___ and ho.

The   hart, the hind and the pret-ty lit - tle doe... ...sing hey___ and ho.

Eventually T. sings the text with S. response. The finger snap, which served as a rhythmic placeholder, is eliminated. When process is secure, T. switches parts with S. Students at this point should know and be able to sing the entire melody.

Before attempting to sing this song in a 3-part canon, the teacher must be sure that the tune is sung accurately. The highlighted notes in the version above indicate where the most problems occur. Address the clarification of these notes by using the "instant fermata" technique to isolate these problem pitches (described below).

Instant Fermata Technique
Have students slowly sing the melody in rhythm. When a problem pitch is reached, T. snaps fingers or claps hands to indicate that S. should place an "instant fermata" on the problem pitch. Discrepancies among the group can then be addressed. During subsequent singings, repeat the "instant fermata" technique, tuning up the problem pitch while sustaining. With a second T. snap or clap, the melody continues on in rhythm.

As with many Renaissance canons, the canonic entrance may occur after various time intervals. This example indicates the canonic entrance after 6 beats. It will also enter after 3 beats.

DIVERGENT EXERCISES
The nature of a strictly composed canon such as *Hey, Ho, to the Greenwood* does not allow for flexible interpretations or improvisations. Divergent activities can be centered on the phrase structure of the melody students learned through the previous teaching-processes. Challenge students to create contrasting canonic movement that addresses the similarities and differences in each phrase.

1. Choreograph a simple contradance-like step pattern that will be repeated for each "sing hey and ho" repetition.
2. Now devise locomotor movement that reflects the 8-pulse, 5-pulse, 5-pulse patterns that precede each of the repeated "sing hey and ho" refrains.
3. Find ways that the new choreography can function canonically with the three canonic voices sounding simultaneously.

2. La Danse

Quickly

Steven Calantropio

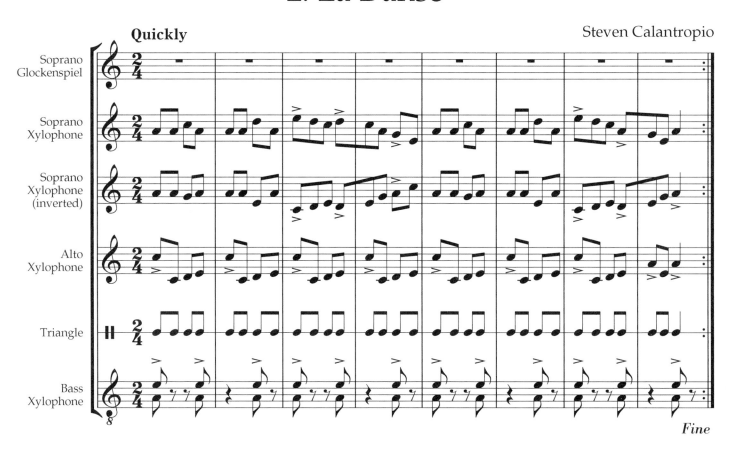

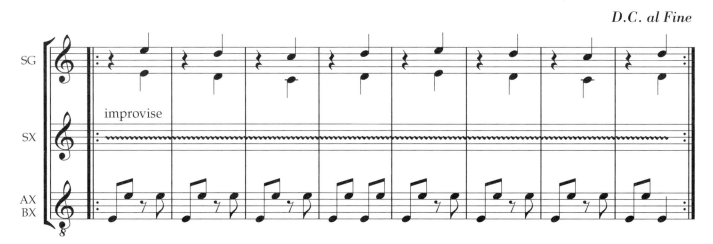

La Danse is so named because it explores the *La*-pentatonic idiom built upon the tonic pitch "A." The rhythmic interplay between the parts should stimulate improvisations by both SX and AX players that are basically rhythmic in nature for the B section. Encourage improvisers to consider the elements of the A section as part of their improvisations.

EXPLORATION

Begin by exploring state names that contains four syllables. Then find any names composed of three, two or one syllable. NOTE: Avoid any name that uses an anacrusis or upbeat, unaccented first syllable; (for example, A-LAS -ka, Ver-MONT, etc.). For this exercise, we will use Massachusetts, Idaho, Texas and Maine. Have S. simultaneously recite the names in rhythm as T. points to them .

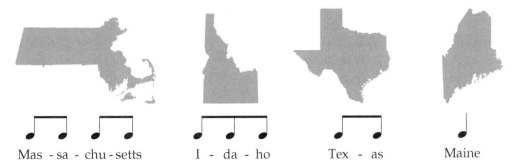

Mas - sa - chu - setts   I - da - ho   Tex - as   Maine

Next, have students study the graphic "score" below and recite the entire pattern, being sure to stress the first syllable of each name. Once secure, creative students may wish to create a body percussion version of the rhythm.

Transfer this rhythm to barred instruments that have been prepared in *La*-pentatonic on A by removing the F and B bars. Using the suggested R–L sticking pattern will help in playing the melody. Be sure that students observe the accented first syllable of each name. Slowly, demonstrate each new melodic state name pattern adding it cumulatively to the previously learned ones.

R L R L   R L R L   R L R L   R L *sim.*   R L R

Once the melody is learned, invite students to explore the concept of diaphony or "mirror image" melodic movement. As the melody moves in one direction, the diaphonic part moves in the opposite direction. Have students work out the diaphonic mirror of the melody. Using two players or groups of players, have them perform the parts together.

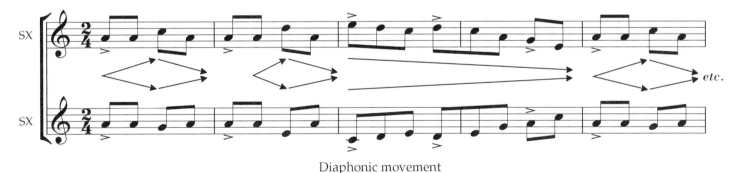

Diaphonic movement

Preparing the Accompaniment:
Again using the names of states, have students create a speech ostinato (below) using a state name with three sounds (ex. Mi-chi-gan) and two sounds (ex. Kan-sas)

Mich - i - gan   Kan - sas   Mich - i - gan   Mich - i - gan   Kan - sas

Call the students' attention to the accented first sound of each word. Have them speak only the first sound of the state names in the pattern above omitting the second and third sounds and simultaneously patting both L and R knees.

Mich - i - gan   Mich - i - gan   Kan - sas

Transfer the knee patting to the BX using the drone pitches of A and E. Have students perform the BX ostinato with the melody played on SX to experience the cross accents between the parts.

etc.

Prepare the AX ostinato by suggesting that students try playing the four syllable name "A-la-ba-ma" as an ascending ostinato starting on low C (#1). As the name has only four syllables and the pentatonic scale has five pitches, ask them to skip over the note G so that the pattern ends each time on A (#2). Finally, as the state name Alabama begins with the letter A, ask them to start the pattern on the pitch A (#3). Cadence the pattern to A at the last pitch of the melody (as scored). Ask a tambourine player to also play the "A-la-ba-ma" rhythm throughout this process.

#1   #2   #3

AX   AX   AX

Preparing the B section:
A second ostinato must be learned by the alto xylophone players. Again using state names, have students echo the following speech pattern:

U - tah,   A - las - ka,   New Jer - sey   and   Min - ne - so - ta,   Wash-ing- ton.

When secure, transfer the speech pattern to patschen as follows:

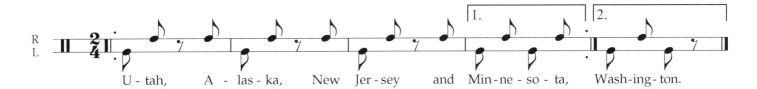

U - tah,   A - las - ka,   New Jer - sey   and Min - ne - so - ta,   Wash-ing- ton.

Now transfer the patschen gestures to octave E pitches on the AX/BX (as scored). As AX/BX plays this ostinato, ask the remaining students to snap their fingers in the space between each of the first three state names in the speech pattern. Transfer this finger snap to octave E pitches on the glockenspiels. When the rhythmic placement of this part is secure, ask students to begin to move the pitch in a repetitive stepwise melody down to C and back to E again as scored below:

DIVERGENT EXERCISES
Improvising a B section

With the B section accompaniments in place, students can attempt to create some melodic improvisations over these patterns. As suggested in the opening chapters of this book, melodic improvisation should begin with some exploration of musical ideas already found in the model. Looking at the A section, one finds:

- an ascending and descending melody in A *La*-pentatonic
- cross accents between the the melody and alto xylophone ostinato
- a constant eighth note feel with embedded syncopations

Ask improvisers to begin their creations by simply playing quarter note ascending and descending patterns. Then develop these patterns both rhythmically and melodically. As the B section revolves around the dominant pitch E , their creations should attempt to reinforce this pitch as an intermediate tonal center. With the B section repeated, there are a total of 32 beats of music to improvise; this can be broken down into two repeated 'tunes' of 16 beats each.

3. To Work Upon the Railway

Irish-American Folk Song

Fil - i - mee-oo - ree oo - ree ay,   Fil - i - mee-oo - ree   oo - ree ay,

Fil - i - mee-oo - ree   oo - ree ay, to work u - pon the rail - way.

This rollicking American folk-song clearly has Irish roots. It can be performed with a soloist dramatizing the verses while all sing the chorus. The refrain can be performed on recorders while singers perform an original line dance. The transcontinental railroad was considered the greatest American engineering feat of the 19th century. It was completed on May 10, 1869 with the driving of a railroad spike of pure gold at Promontory Summit, Utah. The bulk of the workers who built the railroad were Irish and Chinese immigrants.

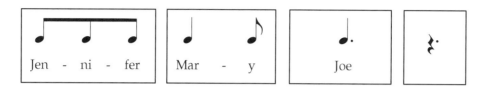

EXPLORATION

1. Explore the three names and rest (above) through simultaneous imitation. Each symbol lasts for one beat of compound meter time. As T. touches each card, students speak the name. Next ask students to remember and repeat a pattern on cards after touching them in rhythm (cards can be repeated, not all cards need be used). This creates a four-beat phrase. Ask S. to create their own four-beat phrases and repeat them three times. Now, create a different, contrasting pattern to answer the three repetitions. This creates a small rhythmic form: A-A-A-B. Transfer student patterns to patschen and then transfer individual rhythm patterns to unpitched percussion instruments (conga, bongo, temple blocks).

2. Create a body percussion accompaniment for these student improvisations using two alternating BP patterns:

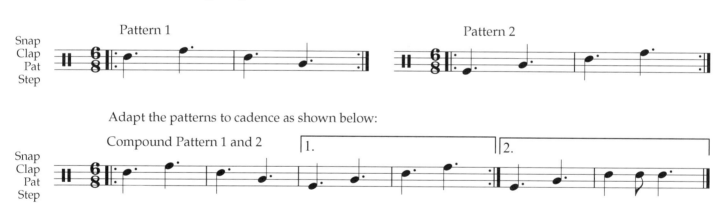

Adapt the patterns to cadence as shown below:

3. Reminding students of the A-A-A-B structure of their improvisations, have them speak the "work" rhythms below at first individually and then as two simultaneous rhythms:

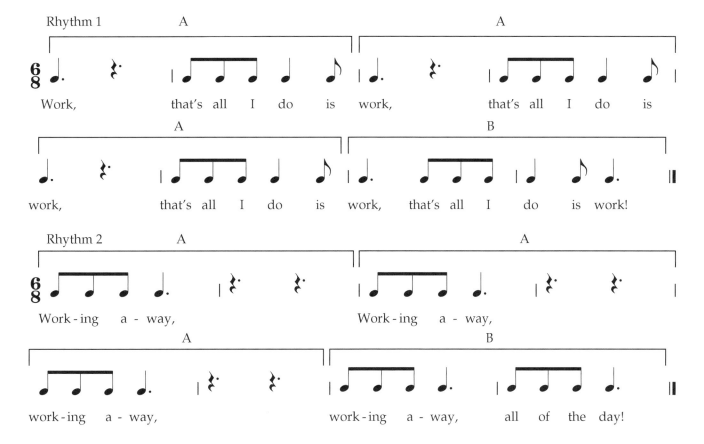

Rhythm 1

Work, that's all I do is work, that's all I do is

work, that's all I do is work, that's all I do is work!

Rhythm 2

Work-ing a - way, Work-ing a - way,

work-ing a - way, work-ing a - way, all of the day!

4. Transfer the compound body percussion accompaniment (previous page) to the bass xylophone. Once secure, adapt the pattern by adding in the passing notes (circled) and changing the rhythm of the final measure. Encourage students to use the L–R sticking indicated which will make the pattern easier to play.

BX

L R L R R L R L R L R L R R L R L R

5. Transfer work rhythm #1 to the alto xylophone. The part is played only on the low E which is one of the common tones between the tonic and mediant triads in Aeolian mode. Work rhythm # 2 is played on temple blocks. Encourage the performer to play each phrase on a different block. The AX and TB parts work together in complementary rhythm.

AX

TB

AX

TB

6. The glockenspiel part is introduced through a body percussion pattern:

Remind students of the first melodic pattern of the familiar song *Hot Cross Buns* (mi-re-do). The pattern can be played from a number of starting points on the instrument. Ask glockenspiel players to play the pattern simultaneously with the three finger snaps starting on high E as the rest of the class performs the BP pattern. Discuss the concept of inverting the pattern (do-re-mi). The task is now to play the pattern in its original form alternating with the inverted version.

Now ask players to play on the two claps of the BP pattern. They play a high C and low A followed by the previously learned pattern.

7. The refrain of the song is easily learned on soprano recorder. Invite students to echo the melodic configurations (below) and slowly adapt them by adding repeated, passing, lower and upper neighbor tones.

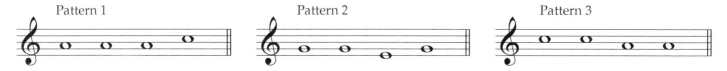

Sequential adaptations for pattern #1 are shown. Devise others for patterns 2 and 3.

8. A final performance of this song might include a soloist who performs the verses in costume while the chorus and dancers sing the refrain. The refrain can be sung and then followed by recorders while dancers perform in opposing lines. Students can improvise A-A-A-B melodies based upon the earlier rhythmic

improvisations they created at the start of the lesson. For melodic improvisation, limit the tonality to *La*-pentatonic on A to eliminate the 1/2 steps that can occur in Aeolian. The *La*-pentatonic scale sounds fine with both the tonic triad (A minor) and the mediant triad (C Major)

Divergent Exercises

The elemental form A-A-A-B is commonly found in music from Ireland. Although not part of *Work Upon the Railway* the repeated A section can imply a melodic sequence. It is often text related. Consider the closing stanza from American poet T.S. Eliot's *The Hollow Men*:

> This is the way the world ends
> This is the way the world ends
> This is the way the world ends
> Not with a bang but a whimper.

Many children's folk-songs begin with a two-line rhyming couplet that is developed into A-A-A-B form through repetition of the first line:

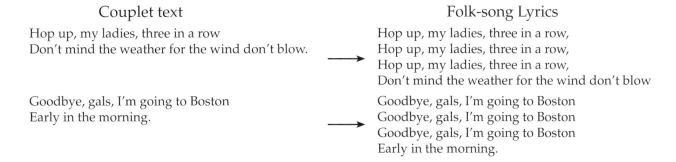

Couplet text	Folk-song Lyrics
Hop up, my ladies, three in a row Don't mind the weather for the wind don't blow.	Hop up, my ladies, three in a row, Hop up, my ladies, three in a row, Hop up, my ladies, three in a row, Don't mind the weather for the wind don't blow
Goodbye, gals, I'm going to Boston Early in the morning.	Goodbye, gals, I'm going to Boston Goodbye, gals, I'm going to Boston Goodbye, gals, I'm going to Boston Early in the morning.

Ask students to create their own A-A-A-B structures both in speech, rhythm and melody.

Ask students to create augmented rhythmic and melodic A-A-A-B patterns where each section is twice as long (8 beats) and the entire structure is 32 beats long.

4. Raspberries

Ukranian Folk-song

This delightful Ukrainian melody gives students the opportunity to play in the minor mode. The syncopation patterns found in the orchestration give the lesson another conceptual focus.

1. Rhythmic Exploration

Explain to S. that in this lesson, the three syllable words "rasp-ber-ry" and "blue-ber-ry" are spoken with two different rhythms:

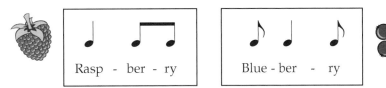

To familiarize students with the rhythmic vocabulary found in this arrangement, T. dictates rhythms from drum using different combinations of the words. Students must answer in speech. Also add in "pear," "apple," and "watermelon" rhythms. Use various rhythms from the score asking students to first echo in speech, then echoing with clapping or rhythm sticks.

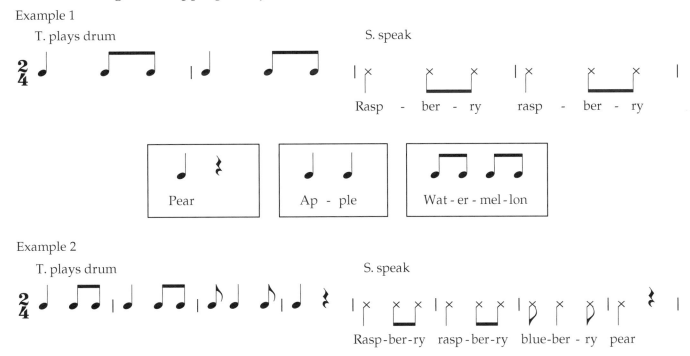

2. Teaching the Melody

• A section (Verse):

T speaks first two bars (call), students speak second bar twice more as a response:
    (T): Lads and lasses, come along ....(S) come along, come along.
T. points out the textual variation of this pattern in the second line of the second verse:
    (T): One for me and one for you ....(S) one for *me*, one for *you.*
T. now sings call, while students speak response. When secure switch parts with students. Complete the process by now asking S. to sing entire verse melody

• B section (Chorus)
 T. sings melody in 4 two-bar phrases asking "which are melodically the same"?
(none). S.continue echoing different melodic patterns until the B section is secure.

3. Learn the Orchestration

Students should be aware at all times that the Verse and Chorus of the song have different accompaniment patterns.

- Bass Xylophone: Verse

Dictate the following patschen pattern, slowly morphing it to the verse BX pattern using the three steps below:

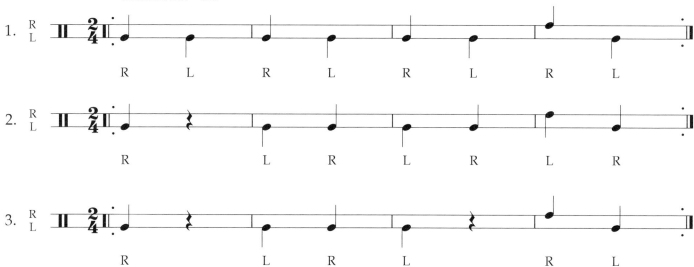

When secure, transfer the patschen pattern to the notes E and B as scored.

T. now dictates the following melodic patterns for S. to echo on barred instruments. T. slowly adapts the pattern moving from version 1 to 2 to 3. The becomes the BX pattern for the chorus.

- AX: Verse

Have S. count the number of beats in the verse without the repetition (8). As T. sings verse, ask students to "count and walk" down eight bars of their instruments starting on high G. Repeat again. The becomes the AM part for the Verse only.

- AX: Verse

Ask S. to sing the verse of the song while patting the thighs with both hands in the rhythm indicated. Transfer this rhythm to AX pitches E and B as scored.

- AX: Chorus

Prepare the AX and tambourine rhythms of the chorus using the "blueberry" rhythm explored earlier in the lesson. Other fruit names are used for the first and second endings.

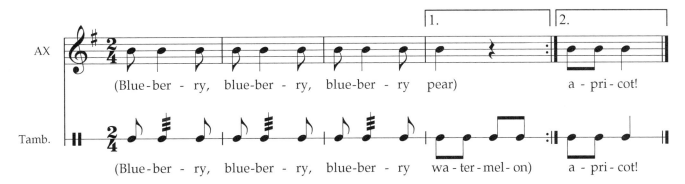

- AG: Chorus

The alto glockenspiel part can be learned cumulatively. Explain that you will freely sing the first note of the five notes found in AG pattern. Students must find the sung note (B) and play it. T. then sings first and second note which S. adds to the first. This continues for all five notes. When they are learned, T. sings the part in rhythm. S. echo on their instruments.

(teacher sings; students play)

Students may enjoy singing the verse in 3-part harmony as a culmination to the arrangement.

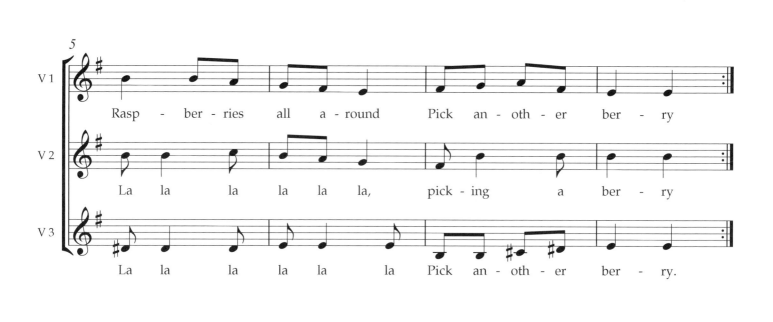

5. Spring Carol

Tempus Adeste Floridum
from *Piae Cantiones*, 1582

1. Spring has now un-wrapped the flow'rs,   day   is   fast   re - viv   -   ing.

Life,   in   all   her   grow - ing pow'rs   towards the   light   is   striv   -   ing.

Gone the i-ron touch of cold win-ter time and frost time.

Seed-lings work-ing through the mold, Now make up for lost____ time.

2. Through each wonder of fair days, God himself expresses.
Beauty follows all His ways, as the world He blesses.
So, as He renews the earth, artist without rival,
In His grace of glad new birth, we must seek revival.

3. Praise the maker all ye saints, He with glory girt you
He who skies and meadows paints, fashioned all your virtue.
Praise Him seers, heroes, kings, heralds of perfection,
Brothers, praise Him for He brings all to resurrection!

Few people know that the melody of the familiar holiday melody *Good King Wenceslas* was originally composed as the *Spring Carol* in a collection of secular and sacred songs from 1582 titled *Piae Cantiones*. The playability of the tune combined with the joyous text make this arrangement a welcome addition to any Spring concert. By engaging children and adults in ritual-based song and dance activities in praise of nature's re-awakening, we reaffirm humanity's common joy at the possibilities of rebirth on all levels.

EXPLORATION

It is quite possible that children will already know the melody from hearing it performed as *Good King Wenceslas*. Nevertheless, the following process will give students insight into the structure of the tune which will assist them in understanding the orchestration.

Have children explore the two texts (below); one a traditional rhyme and the other an original corollary. Divide S. into two groups; one group speaks the first rhyme followed by the other speaking the second.

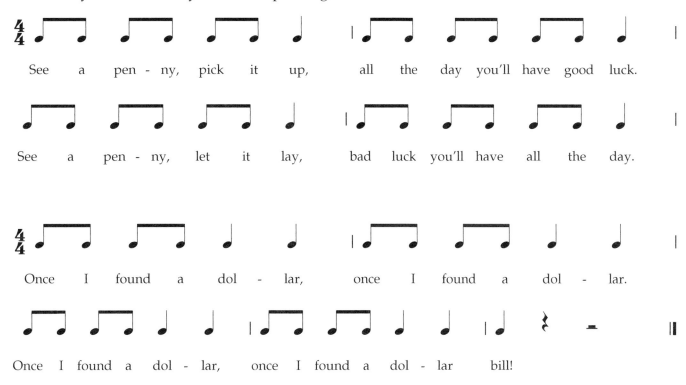

Using a process called interleaving, have the first group of students speak the first measure of their text followed by the second group reciting the first measure of their text. Continue this process to the end of the second text. Once the interleaving process is secure have all students speak the merged version of the two texts:

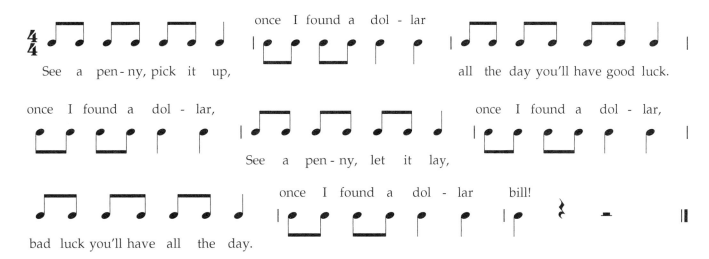

Ask students to sing the interleaved measures of the second text using the melodic pattern as a response to the T.'s singing of the text 1 measures. The students will need to adapt the last two measures of their text to accommodate the developing melody. Have students and teacher switch parts; at this point S. should know the entire melody.

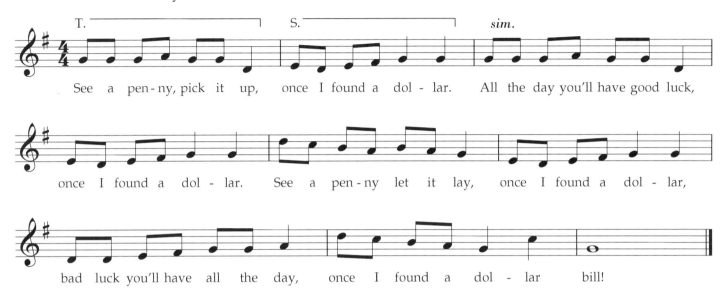

See a pen-ny, pick it up, once I found a dol-lar. All the day you'll have good luck,
once I found a dol-lar. See a pen-ny let it lay, once I found a dol-lar,
bad luck you'll have all the day, once I found a dol-lar bill!

NOTE: The accommodation of the last two bars of the tune will need to be addressed in each of the instrument parts of the orchestration as well. It is the extra measure of the fourth phrase that gives the melody its distinctive character. Students should understand that it must be accommodated in all learning from this point forward.

It is now a simple matter of substituting the original text for the ones used to learn the tune. *The Oxford Book of Carols* (Oxford University Press, reprinted 1985) which names this song the *Flower Carol*, offers five verses for the melody. I have selected verses 1, 3 and 5 for this arrangement renaming them verses 1 , 2 and 3.

Verse 1:
Spring has now unwrapped the flowers, day is fast reviving.
Life in all her growing powers towards the light is striving.
Gone the iron touch of cold. Winter time and frost time,
Seedlings, working through the mold, now make up for lost time

Verse 2:
Through each wonder of fair days, God Himself expresses.
Beauty follows all His ways as the world He blesses.
So, as He renews the earth, artist without rival.
In His grace of glad new birth, we must seek revival

Verse 3:
Praise the Maker, all ye saints, He with glory girt you.
He, who skies and meadows paints, fashioned all your virtue.
Praise Him, seers, heroes, kings, heralds of perfection.
Brothers, praise Him for He brings all to resurrection!

Teaching the Orchestration: BX AX AM

Begin teaching the BX part by pointing out the harmonic patterns of the four phrases. Only the tonic and subdominant triads are used to harmonize the melody except for one instance of the dominant triad used on the last beat of measure 7. As mentioned previously, accommodating this brief harmonic change along with the extension of the ninth measure will require careful student attention.

Teacher dictates the body percussion pattern in A example (below) with all students singing the text (sing "I" as "one," "IV" as "four" and "V" as "five"). Ask BX players to play the pattern as everyone else sings, playing the chord roots for I (G), IV (C) and V (D) as written. They must play A example three times in a row before moving to the more rhythmic B version and finally the more melodic C version.

Now introduce the D version pointing out that the word "five" indicates the one time change to dominant harmony on that beat. After some practice, students will understand the "translation" of the body percussion patterns into pitched chord roots. Now the entire accompaniment can be performed by repeating the C pattern 3 times followed by the D pattern. Ask students to play or sing the melody while the BX players perform their part.

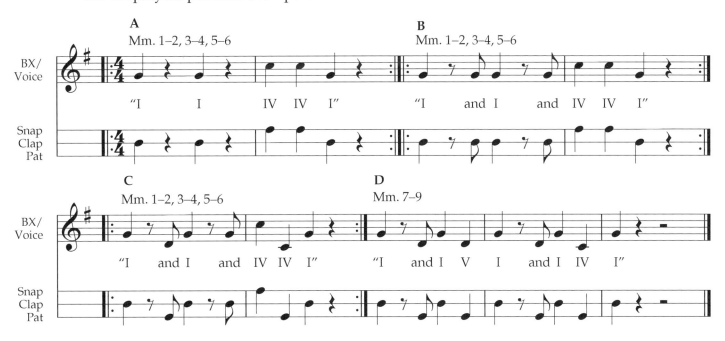

Prepare the AX part in much the same way as the BX. Begin by having students imitate the body percussion A pattern (below). It must be performed three times in a row. While students are learning this pattern, have AX players substitute a harmonic fourth D-G on any clapping and a harmonic fifth C-G for any patschen. Beginning a rhythm pattern on the second eighth note of a measure is a challenge. AX players may wish to click their two mallet sticks together to indicate the strong beats (steps) followed by the played intervals, eventually eliminating the mallet click when secure.

T. demonstrates the B pattern below for the fourth phrase. Students play a harmonic fifth D–A where the finger snaps occur. The patschen in measure 8 (highlighted) is adapted to a harmonic third E–C.

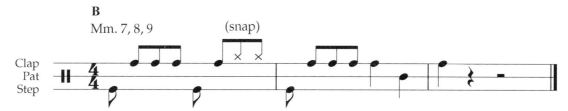

NOTE: Clearly this is a challenging part and care should be taken not to rush the teaching process. Be certain that the body percussion patterns are clear and performed accurately before moving students to the instruments. Add speech to the rhythm, create a little game out of it and do whatever else is necessary to insure that students have significant experience with the part before assigning it to the instrument. Once assigned, be sure to have the BX play along to provide the downbeat for the AX. Eventually perform this AX part with the singing or playing of the melody.

While the interplay between the BX and AX parts is somewhat complex, the orchestration is stabilized by the alto metallophone pattern which moves strictly to the pulse. Begin with reviewing the arpeggiated bordun pattern (A) which is quite familiar to students who regularly play these instruments:

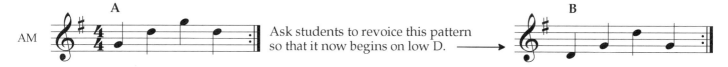

Ask students to revoice this pattern so that it now begins on low D. ⟶

Adapt every second pattern by changing the starting pitch to low C (circled); the rest of the pattern remains the same. Repeat three times:

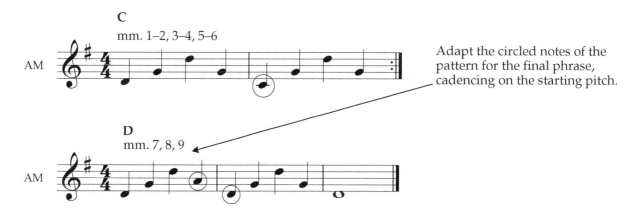

Adapt the circled notes of the pattern for the final phrase, cadencing on the starting pitch.

The glockenspiel countermelody can be taught the way many melodies are taught. Begin with a simplified version of the tune using melodic configurations without rhythm and slowly adapt them, adding in passing and neighboring tones and finally playing in rhythm. Have S. play the repeated bars of the countermelody (measures 1, 3, 5, 7) considering it a "question" with four different answers played by T. Whenever possible, use a type of notational "shorthand" to keep the actual music reading to a minimum, while encouraging S. to watch and listen closely:

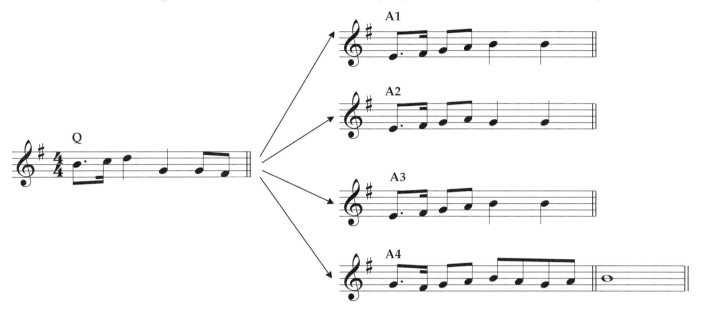

Performance Suggestions for the Spring Carol

Being elemental in nature, the melody of the Spring Carol can be accompanied by a simple drone pattern. You may wish to accompany the first verse with a drone accompaniment as suggested below:

You may choose to create an additive arrangement, adding the orchestrated BX, AX and AM patterns during verse 2 and completing the orchestration with the addition of the glockenspiel countermelody on verse 3

The following two measure pattern for BX and glockenspiels can serve as an introduction, interlude or coda:

Because the melody is quite playable on soprano recorders, singers can alternate between singing and dancing while a small group of recorder players play the melody with orchestration. Have students create the dance patterns, using the added extra measure in the fourth phrase for some kind of flourish or cadence figure

The following is one suggestion for a performance sequence that I have used successfully with children:

Introduction	Verse 1	Interlude	Verse 2
BX, SG, AG, Tri.	BX, AM, G, with drone	BX, SG, Ag, Tri.	BX, Ax, Am, orchestrated
Dance w. SR	**Interlude**	**Verse 3**	**Coda**
BX, AX, AM add G cm.	BX, SG, AG, Tri.	BX, AX, AM, w. G cm.	BX, SG, AG, Tri.

Advanced choral groups may wish to sing any of the verses in three part paraphony. This choral version can also be played using two soprano recorders on the V.1 and V.2 lines and an alto recorder on the V.3 line. A soloist may also enjoy learning the first verse in the original latin.

Verse 1:
Tempus adest floridum, surgent namque flores
Vernales in omnibus, imitantur mores.
Hoc quod frigus laeserat, reperant calores
Cernimus hoc fieri, per multos labores

6. The Farmer's Dance

Traditional Zwiefacher
arranged by Steven Calantropio

When the sleep - ing world be - gins to a - wake, then the farm - er's up, his liv - ing to make And it's off to work so ear - ly at morn, to the fields to sow the wheat and the corn. His

The Farmer's Dance pays homage to the important contributions that farmers make to each generation often with little or no recognition. The melody is an original *zwiefacher* tune to which a new text has been added. The *zwiefacher* is a rustic Bavarian dance that is still practiced in rural areas of Germany, Switzerland and France and by folk dance groups around the world. The music consists of metric patterns of two beats (called "dreher") and three beat measures (called "waltzer") that change often without warning. Pairs of dancers are called upon to pick up the changing metric patterns and respond to them with simple corresponding step patterns holding each other in a hugging posture.

EXPLORATION

Using the high-low sounds of a set of bongo drums or similar instruments, T. invites students to move in two beat and three beat metric patterns using the name Ma-ry (two beats) and Jen-ni-fer (three beats) or some equivalent names. S. must step the strong beat and clap the weak second or third beats as dictated. Once students are listening closely, T. dictates a longer pattern (A): Mary (2x) Jennifer (2X).

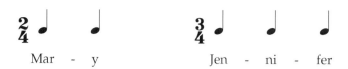

Mar - y   Jen - ni - fer

This entire sequence is done four times. S. practice this pattern until secure and diagram it in a grid template using large strokes for strong beats and smaller strokes for weak beats:

A 4x   **B** 4x

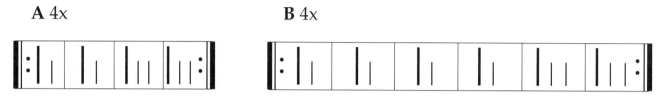

Once this first pattern is secure, another pattern (B) is dictated: Ma-ry (4X) and Jen-ni-fer (2X). This is also performed four times ending with the last strong beat and dropping the remaining two weak beats. Students can perform this extended metric structure in multiple ways:

1. Stepping strong beat and clapping weak beats
2. With a partner, stepping strong beat and patting partner's hands while facing each other
3. With a partner, using the Metric Hand Pattern noted below.

Ask students to come up with other ways to show the strong beat, weak beat metric patterns. For example:

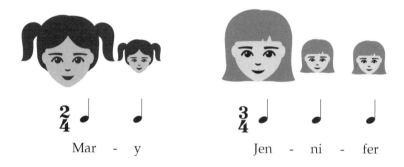

Mar - y   Jen - ni - fer

Metric Hand Pattern

Beat 2: Pat palm of partner's R hand with R hand *above* L.

Beat 1: Pat back of partner's L hand with your R hand.

Beat 2 + 3: Pat palm of partner's R hand with your R hand *below* L.

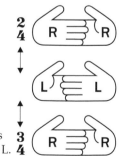

Developing a Dance

Following discussion about a farmer's role in society in the past and present, students now begin to develop a pantomime dance that reflects the life of a farmer from previous times. Ask students to show the gestures that a farmer might have used in his daily work a century or more ago before. These could include planting seed, threshing wheat or hay, picking crops, feeding animals, shoeing a horse, etc.

Using the metric pattern learned previously, invite small groups of students to organize these gestures into a dance by performing them on the strong beats of each measure. The gestures will need to be stylized and somewhat exaggerated to provide a flow of movement from one to the next. Encourage locomotor movement through the A and B patterns along with high and low levels of "work" gestures. Such pantomime dances showing routines of daily life have been around for centuries. T. may assist students work by providing a drum accompaniment or students may choose unpitched percussion to organize an accompaniment by articulating two and three beat measures.

T. asks S. to perform the A and B sections of the metric pattern learned previously using knee patting and clapping:

As students perform, T. sings melody of *The Farmer's Dance*. When secure, switch parts with T. performing body percussion part while students sing:

- **Learning the Orchestration—BX**

Earlier, students had stepped and clapped the strong and weak beats of the two changing metric patterns. Now ask students to clap only on the strong beats while singing the melody. T. dictates changes from tonic harmony (clapped) to dominant harmony (knee patting). Playing with the left hand only, transfer the tonic strong beats to the note G on bass xylophones and the dominant strong beats to the low D. With the right hand, play a high D with each of the left hand pitches. This outlines both the metric and harmonic structures of the A and B sections (see below) and becomes the BX part as scored.

AX : Ask students to review the hand clap/knee pat pattern learned previously. Now ask them to invert the pattern changing claps to pats and pats to claps.

Transfer all claps to the pitch G on alto xylophones. Transfer all knee pats to low D. Now, listening closely to where the BX changes to the dominant pitch, AX mirrors this melodic movement by changing their G to an F♯ and returning to G when the bass line returns to the tonic pitch.

Glockenspiels: A section: Ask the BX and AX to play their parts together. Challenge other students to clap their hands 3 times in rhythm followed by a finger snap when the first pair of 3/4 measures are reached, doing so each time a 3/4 bar follows a 2/4 bar. Dictate the first glockenspiel pattern (G-A-B-D) alternating with the second (D-E-F♯-G), repeating this entire line twice as it follows the A section metric scheme.

Glockenspiels: B section: Ask the glockenspiel players to sing the song fragment "noble work, never done" from the melody of the B section. After isolating and playing it on their instruments, invite them to play the same pattern in paraphony a harmonic third below, explaining how the melody will be harmonized in parallel thirds. Play the same pattern with the melodic fragment "in his joy, feeds the world":

The melody can also be sung in three parts and/or played on recorders as indicated below if students' musical abilities allows for this. Try combining unison singing with orchestration followed by a selected farmer's dance with recorder accompaniment and then the three part vocal arrangement with barred instruments and recorders for a full performance version of this delightful tune!

Divergent Exercises

Another way to explore time change patterns is to let students create their own metric structures based on geometrical shapes. Consider the following shapes with the meters and rhythms implied by their names:

Assign a color for a harmonic change (I-V, I - VII, etc):

Light shading = Tonic Harmony   Dark shading = Alternate Harmony

Create phrase patterns using various shapes and colors.

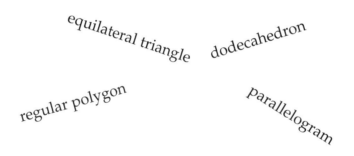

Find other shapes with more varied name rhythms.

equilateral triangle   dodecahedron

regular polygon   parallelogram

7. Hushabye

American Folk-song

The American composer Aaron Copland (1900–1990) considered *Hushabye* one of the finest examples of folk-songs. He included it in his second collection of *Old American Songs* (1952) under the title *The Little Horses*. The lyrical melody in Aeolian mode allows for melodic improvisation using changing triads over a tonic drone.

Learning the Song

Begin by asking students to sing the Aeolian mode on E both ascending and descending using whatever scale degree names they are familiar with (*La*-tonic, *Do*-Minor tonic, fixed *Do*, scale degree numbers, etc.) or just with neutral syllables ("loo, lai," etc.). Next T. sings the ascending pattern and students answer with the descending pattern. See examples. Caution singers to keep the descending scale in tune as the tendency of singing descending intervals flat must be avoided. During these exercises, the bass metallophone can roll a low E to help with intonation.

The teacher's ascending pattern is removed and students sing their descending pattern (example 1). S. now eliminate the upper tonic note and begin the descending pattern on the seventh scale degree D. The upper tonic note which was "removed" is now sung as a lower tonic at the end of the pattern (highlighted notes in examples 1 & 2). T. claps the rhythm of the text of measures 3 & 4 and students sing the descending pattern in that rhythm. Students substitute the four text phrases for the neutral syllables they have been singing (example 3). T. sings the first two bars of each phrase which are answered by the students. T. and S. switch parts; finally students sing the entire melody.

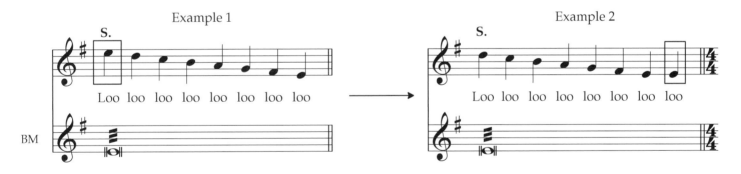

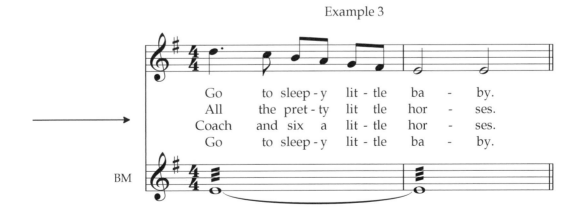

. . . Go to sleepy little baby.
. . . All the pretty little horses.
. . . Coach and six a little horses.
. . . Go to sleepy little baby

Slowly

Hush - a - bye, don't you cry, go to sleep-y lit - tle ba - by.

When you wake you shall have all the pret - ty lit - tle hors - es.

Blacks and bays, dap-ples and grays, coach and six a lit - tle hors - es.

Hush - a - bye, don't you cry, go to sleep-y lit - tle ba - by.

Learning the Orchestration

Begin by learning the bass metallophone part. Students imitate T. patting a pulse on the L. knee with the L. hand. Introduce the text; "Now I will sing you a lullaby" which is patted in rhythm on the R. knee simultaneously. Have the hands rest for 1 beat after the word lullaby before repeating the pattern.

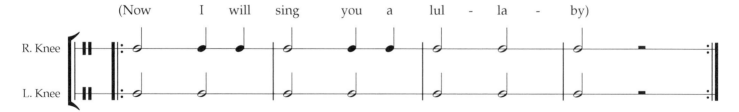

(Now I will sing you a lul - la - by)

R. Knee

L. Knee

Once secure, T. explains the concept of musical augmentation where, in this case, the lengths of all notes are doubled and the speed of the pattern is half as fast as before.

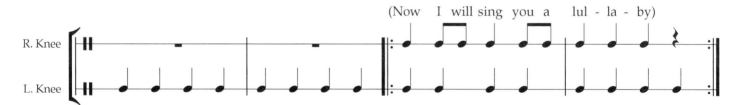

(Now I will sing you a lul - la - by)

R. Knee

L. Knee

Once secure, students can transfer this pattern to E and B. The upper voice "B" moves up one pitch to "C" on the text "sing you a..." moving to A for two half notes before returning to B for the rest of the pattern. (Note: If the rhythm is too challenging for one individual,this part can be performed by two players on two instruments or even on the same instrument.)

To teach the alto metallophone part, ask students to observe and describe the following two melodic configurations:

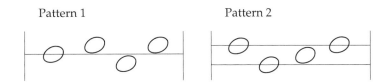

Question students about how these two patterns may be played if they began on the note G. Invite students to play pattern 1 (in rhythm as scored) twice followed by pattern 2 twice with the same note value:

Prepare the finger cymbal part by snapping fingers where the asterisk occurs in the AM example above. The part acts as a connector between phrases. Transfer to finger cymbals when secure.

Again, call students' attention to the descending melodic phrase discussed earlier in the lesson process. Explain that two melodies sound well together when they move in opposite directions, called contrary motion. Ask them to play an ascending melodic line beginning on F♯ using the same text and rhythm as the descending line (lower part, example 1). Have two players or groups play or sing them simultaneously. Now simplify the ascending line using the text "Hush, lit-tle Ba-by" on the first three repetitions (lower part , example 2) . On the fourth phrase, the text rhythm becomes "Hush MY lit-tle ba-by" (example 3).

The song is ready for a performance which can include a hummed verse, a soloist singing the calls, while all sing the responses, or new call verses made up by the performers.

Divergent Exercises

Invite students to improvise new melodies above the harmonic sequence of *Hushabye* by carefully guiding them through the following four step sequence:

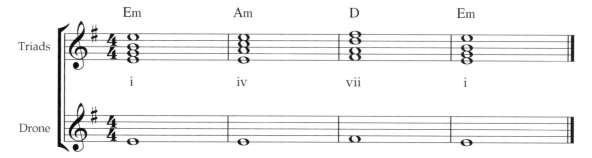

Step 1:

Ask students playing soprano or tenor recorders to play one note of the starting triad and follow it by stepwise movement or repetition to its closest neighbor in each consecutive chord. This can be done over an accompaniment of BM, AM and FC using the ostinato pattern from the song orchestration.

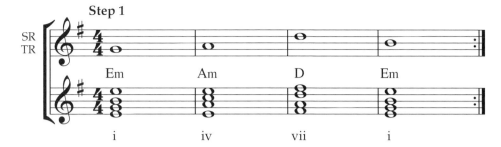

Step 2:

Next select two different notes of each triad, skipping from the first and second of each triad in half note rhythm.

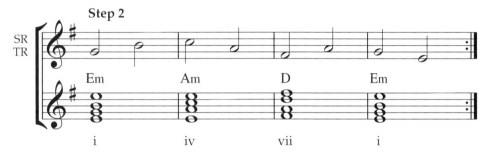

Step 3:

The third step in the improvisation is to begin to connect the two notes using quarter note rhythms and passing from one chord tone to another. The passing from triad to triad can be accomplished through repetition, stepwise movement or through a small intervallic skip.

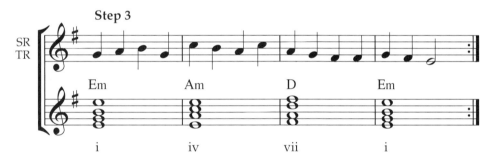

Step 4:

Finally, students will need to freely move from chord to chord tone using varied rhythms to create a melodic line. Review the concepts of what creates a fine melody (predominantly stepwise movement, melodic patterns, use of patterns in rhythm and melody, cadencing on tonic pitch, etc.). This exercise is a great step towards one of the most satisfying of musical experiences: improvising melodies over harmonic progressions. Allow opportunities to improvise over multiple class periods for students to understand and feel comfortable with the process.

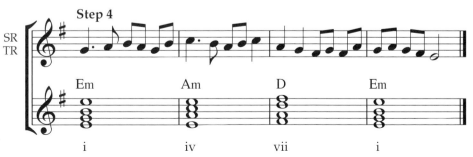

8. Somebody's Waiting for Me

American Play Party

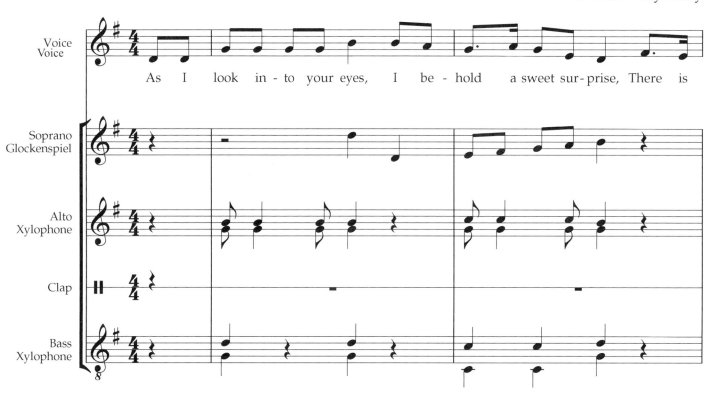

As I look in-to your eyes, I be-hold a sweet sur-prise, There is

some - bod - y wait - ing for me.

Children and adults enjoy this simple play party game. Early American play parties were actually dances that were given this name to circumvent strict religious objections to traditional "dancing." Although play parties were usually sung with little or no accompaniment, the appealing melody of *Somebody's Waiting* provides an opportunity for students to explore a I - IV - V functional harmony setting on the barred instruments.

Play Party Directions

Formation: Dancers in a circle holding hands. One person is in the center of the circle.

A Section: (This section is sung only once)
As the first section of the song is sung ("As I look into your eyes..."), the circle moves counterclockwise. The person in the center of the circle moves clockwise keeping close to the edge of the rotating circle.

B Section: (This section is sung three times)
1st time: ("There is somebody waiting...") Circle and person in the circle continue rotating.

2nd time: ("Take two , leave the others...") Circle stops rotating, all face center. The person in the center takes two persons who have stopped closest to him/her and brings both to the center of the circle. All clap hands while singing.

3rd time: ("Swing one, leave the other...") Person in center swings one of the "chosen" two; both persons swinging join the circle at the end of this section. Remaining "chosen" person now begins the game again.

Exploration

In the key of G major, ask S. to echo and sing the roots of triad patterns using the tonic, subdominant and dominant triads dictated by T. They indicate the triads using a finger snap for tonic, a knee pat for subdominant and a clap for dominant triads. Eventually, ask students to perform the patterns below, singing the triad roots and indicating the proper body percussion gestures.

   Moving to the barred instruments, ask students to play the A and B patterns with L hand only using the lower G, C and D bars. When secure, add the R hand BX note pair pitches (see below). Students should be able to move freely between the three triads. Point out the larger triads in the two patterns. S. should now perform only the larger triads in both sections.

NOTE: In this lesson, the dominant triad is referred to as both "V" and "V7." Although dominant seventh triads are not ordinarily used in elemental style, an exception is made in this arrangement.

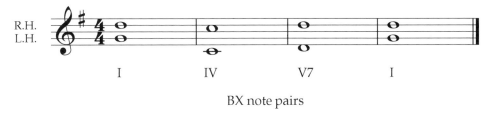

BX note pairs

The bass xylophone A section pattern is played exactly as it has been prepared above. The B section pattern is adapted by having students learn the following speech/patschen pattern:

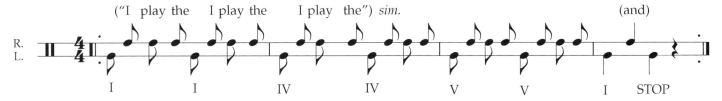

Speak the text both below and above the body percussion staff using alternating hands to perform the patschen pattern. Transfer the pattern to the note pairs. The L hand will play the chord roots indicated by the text below the staff while the R and L play the upper note pair indicated by the text above the staff.

This pattern becomes the bass xylophone part found in the B section:

Teach the alto xylophone part by having students learn 4 pairs of notes:

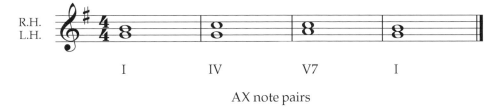

AX note pairs

Ask students to chant the text "Waiting for me" 4 times using the syncopated rhythm indicated in the example (below). Change the text to the triad numbers found below the text. *Be particularly careful of the second repetition where the numeral changes on the word "me."*

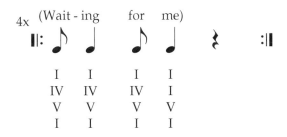

Now apply the triad changes chanted in the previous example to the AX using the AX note pairs. This is the alto xylophone A section and is played once.

In a similar manner, teach the B section for alto xylophone by first inviting students to chant the rhythmic speech (below, upper staff) and then apply the chanted rhythm to the AX note pairs. This is repeated 3 times.

Begin teaching the A section of the glockenspiel countermelody by teaching the following body percussion pattern:

When secure, T. performs the entire pattern while S. isolate and perform the finger snaps only. Transfer the first finger snap pattern to an ascending pentachord beginning on low E. Transfer the second finger snapping pattern to a descending pentachord starting on high D.

1st pattern   2nd pattern

Now ask students to isolate the two hand claps of the body percussion pattern. Transfer these to high D followed by low D. Combine the octave D pattern with the finger snap pentachords. The knee pats are rests; students may silently move mallets in the air to indicate the two rests if necessary. The resultant part is the A section of the glockenspiel countermelody:

The B section of the glockenspiel countermelody can be learned through cumulative dictation. In cumulative dictation, students are given only the first note of a longer pattern which they must find on their instruments. Once all have found this first note, the first and second are dictated sequentially. Students must then play the first and second pitches. This continues through the entire pattern of eight notes.

At first the pitches are played back without strict rhythm. Once all eight pitches are learned, T. can begin to dictate them approximating the scored rhythm using hand claps or finger snaps to show when to proceed to the next pitch.

Cumulative dictation sequence

Once the pitch sequence is secure, T. claps hands in the actual rhythm of the countermelody and students play it back using that rhythm.

Divergent Activities: Melodic Improvisation
Students may enjoy the challenge of improvising over a functional triad progression using tonic, subdominant and dominant triads. The B section of *Somebody's Waiting for Me* provides such an opportunity. Have the bass xylophone and alto xylophone parts serve as an accompaniment to recorder or barred instrument improvisations by repeating the B section accompaniment:

Improvisation Accompaniment

Four Steps to Melodic Improvisation
Over Functional Harmony Changes

1. First have students explore the harmonic progression on the lower staff. Identify triad members (root, 3rd, 5th) in each measure as well as common tones between any two adjacent triads. Next ask them to select a triad member in each measure. Any two consecutive pitches may be a repetition, stepwise movement or a skip away from each other. An example is shown.

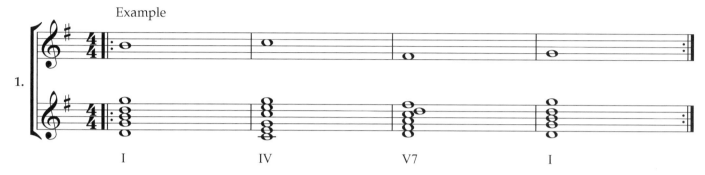

2. Now, keeping their original selections, add a second triad member in each measure. A repeated pitch may be used within a measure or across a barline.

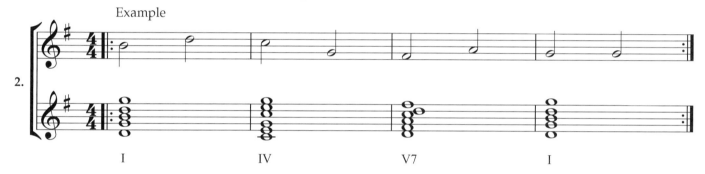

3. The next step is to use four notes above each triad. As these new additions occur on weak beats of the measure they can be non-harmonic passing tones connecting any two triad members or arpeggiated triad members.

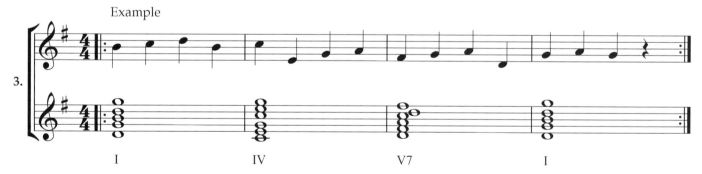

4. Finally, encourage the use of other rhythms, scale patterns, repeated motifs to develop a more melodic phrase. This development is a big leap from the previous so more should be given to developing melodies. The original single pitches can be altered to accommodate more melodic movement. Avoid non-harmonic tones on strong beats; they may certainly be used in passing on weak beats.

Example

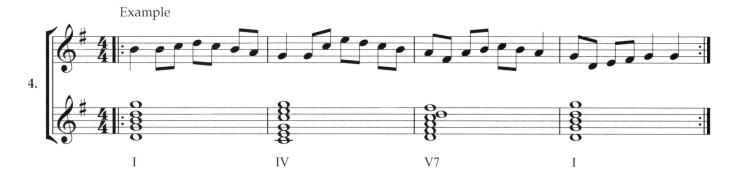

4.

I   IV   V7   I

Give students many opportunities in this improvisatory setting, encouraging them while gently correcting problems. When necessary, go back a step and review the goal of each example. This type of melodic improvisation over harmony changes is a fairly sophisticated process but the resultant music making is quite rewarding for both students and teacher.

9. A Piece of Glass

Steven Calantropio

Do Re Mi Fa Sol____

Do Re Mi Fa Sol____

A Piece of Glass exposes young musicians to the 20th-century minimalist compositional style popularized by composer Philip Glass and others. Minimalism employs continuously repeated patterns that slowly evolve, often with the addition or subtraction of one small element of the original pattern. The technique of phasing is also part of minimalist style. Rhythms and melodic patterns of different lengths played simultaneously move in and out of phase with each other. *A Piece of Glass* uses an adapted 12 measure harmonic pattern similar to traditional blues music.

Exploration

The first skill students will need to master is maintaining a constant eighth note pulse felt in different metric configurations. Use the following traditional texts or parts of texts adapted for this exercise to feel patterns of 7, 6, 5 and 4 eighth notes. Transfer the text to body percussion patterns that the students can create. Ask students to repeat each pattern until secure before moving to the next one. Another exploratory strategy is to assign a small group to each pattern and perform them consecutively, moving from group to group. Create new extended patterns skipping from one to another out of sequence, exploring the texts until all are secure.

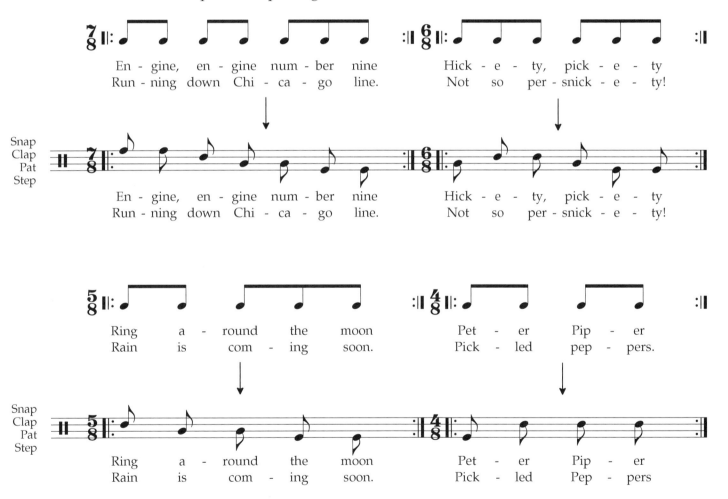

Next, ask students to observe the 12-measure harmonic progression of three triads (below). They will need to memorize this pattern which is similar to a 12-measure blues harmony. The voicings for each triad are given beneath the harmonic scheme. Challenge students to explore these harmonic changes using three mallets (one in the LH and two in the RH). Then ask them to experiment arpeggiating the chord in various configurations using only two mallets.

12-Bar Harmonic Pattern

1	2	3	4		5	6	7	8		9	10	11	12
Am	Am	F	F		Am	Am	F	F		G	F	Am	Am

A simple movement of one note (E) to its upper neighbor (F) facilitates the harmonic movement from A minor to F major. Raising all members of the F major triad one pitch creates the G major triad. This 12-bar pattern never requires a movement from A minor to G major.

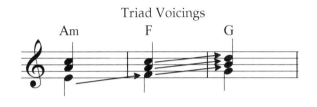
Triad Voicings

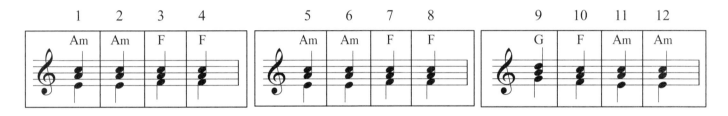

Remind students of the initial steps in this lesson sequence where patterns of 7, 6, 5 and 4 eighth notes were spoken and then performed in body percussion. Beginning with the 7-note pattern ask them to play each measure of the harmonic pattern using the following configuration of the triad members (note: encourage students to use the L-R sticking noted as it will make the performance of the patterns easier).

R L R L R L R

Next try each bar of the harmonic pattern using 6 eighth notes configured as:

L R L R L R

72

Ask students which note of the 7-note pattern has been eliminated to create the 6-note pattern (the 4th note)...

etc.

... and then using 5 eighth notes as follows:

etc.

As a final challenge, ask students to play the entire 12-bar pattern using the following formula:

- All A min. bars are played as: **7** / ♪
- All F maj. bars are played as: **6** / ♪
- All G maj. bars are played as: **5** / ♪

Students may next inquire about the pattern built on 4 eighth notes. This pattern is performed as a repeated ostinato using octave Es articulated on the third eighth note of the pattern, and played along with one of the other patterns which provide the eighth note pulse. It can be layered upon any of the previous 12-bar metric patterns because the number of eighth notes in each metric version is divisible by 4. This repeated E pattern begins at various points in the longer patterns and moves in and out of alignment against them in a technique called phasing.

About phasing. . .

As the glockenspiel ostinato is simultaneously performed with another pattern, it will move in and out of phase with that pattern. Both parts begin together but the starting points of each pattern will move away from each other until they suddenly coincide to begin the phasing pattern again. The length of time that they do not coincide is dictated by the multiple of the two meters. Students may be interested in discovering how many repetition of the glockenspiel ostinato must be played in each meter before the phasing begins again.

7/8 Pattern: 12 bars of 7 meter = 84 eighth notes / 4 eighth note phasing

The glockenspiel pattern will be repeated **21** times:

etc.

6/8 Pattern: 12 bars of 6 meter = 72 eighth notes / 4 eighth note phasing

The glockenspiel pattern will be repeated **18** times:

etc.

5/8 Pattern: 12 bars of 5 meter = 60 eighth notes / 4 eighth note phasing

The glockenspiel pattern will be repeated **15** times:

etc.

Finally, alto and soprano metallophones perform an A min. triad using the following rhythm:

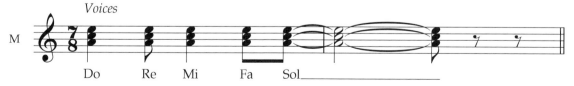

This pattern can be played whenever the two sequential A min. measures begin, regardless of meter (the example above shows the rhythm in 7/8). A group of students can also sing the triad using a fragment of humorous or provocative text. Minimalist style sometimes employs text patterns reduced to a few specific scenic words, eliminating anything considered "non-essential." Any student- or teacher-created idea will work.

Putting it Together

The score of *A Piece of Glass* presented at the start of this lesson is only one possible version of the work. It uses five repetitions of the 12-bar harmonic pattern in various meters and instrumentation. A large suspended gong is lightly struck to initiate each new repetition:

- Repetition 1: Xylophones play 7/8 version
- Repetition 2: Xylophones play 7/8 version adding glockenspiel ostinato (A)
- Repetition 3: Xylophones play 7/8 version with glockenspiels adding metallophone rhythm (B)
- Repetition 4: Xylophones play changing meter version with metallophones; eliminate glockenspiels (C)
- Repetition 5: Xylophones return to 7/8 version with glockenspiel ostinato (D)
- This "modular" type of composition allows students to create new versions of the work by juxtaposing instrumental parts and meters in new combinations.

Divergent Exercises

Ask students to come up with an initial melodic sequence that will be adapted (one melodic and one rhythmic sequence are suggested below). They should consider triad patterns, scale patterns or rhythmic patterns as possible starting points. Develop these motifs by adding or subtracting elements from them. Combine them to make longer patterns. Use a "phasing element" to be played with the original motif and adaptations. Consider raising or lowering the initial motifs by a step.

Melodic Sequence

Phasing Element

Rhythmic Sequence

Phasing Element

10. Lydian Piece

Steven Calantropio

The Lydian mode is characterized by a raised fourth degree which gives it a playful or comical sound. There is very little folk music or composed music that employs this exotic sounding scale. The melody of the *Lydian Piece* emphasizes this characteristic scale degree particularly in the recorder part.

Teaching the Accompaniment
A Section
Begin by demonstrating the body percussion pattern below. Caution students to listen to the entire pattern a number of times before attempting to echo it.

Once secure with the pattern, point out that there are always two sequential hand claps. Ask students to perform only the hand clapping part of the exercise while T. performs the entire rhythm. Moving to the alto xylophones, students can transfer the clapping parts to a harmonic third A/C (#1 below). When they have mastered this rather disjunct rhythm, suggest that they play each pair of eighth notes F/A and A/C (#2 below). Finally, move the A/C third down stepwise on the second pair of eighth notes (#3 below).

Now ask students to perform only the patschen notes of the body percussion rhythm. Suggest that one student transfer this rhythm to the temple blocks. The part creates a "conversation" with the alto xylophone part; neither part "speaks" while the other is playing.

The bass xylophone part functions as a moving bordun and can be taught quite easily using the four steps below.

A: Begin with a simple drone played to the pulse of the music
B: Now rock the upper voice between the notes C and D
C: Begin to alternate the L. and R. hands beginning with L. Now double the speed of the alternating hands alerting students to the idea of diminution in music. This measure is repeated three times.
D: Pattern C is adapted to cadence on the tonic pitch of this Lydian scale (high F)

B Section Accompaniment

Ask students to echo the phrase "Like it, I Like it" as an ostinato repeating it six times and cadencing on "Like." Have some students transfer the speech pattern to patschen. Ask other students to add a finger snap in the space after the word "it:"

Transfer the patschen sounds to octave Cs on alto xylophones. The finger snap is transferred to the temple blocks, choosing various pitched blocks for each snap:

While the accompaniment patterns of the *Lydian Piece* can be taught in a fairly straightforward manner, the melody will need more exploration and preparation. Players will need a significant level of fingering technique to move quickly around the F Lydian scale. The repeated C-B movement, which gives the mode its characteristic sound, will present some fingering challenges.

Begin by introducing some simple patterns found in the A section piece as melodic configurations, being sure students can finger them smoothly and accurately. Do not attempt to play these melodic motifs in rhythm until secure.

Next explore the unique sounds of the mode with some 4-beat improvised question and answer patterns between teacher and students. T should create question patterns that end on the dominant pitch C and use rhythms from the melody while asking students to begin their responses on C and do the same moving to either the high or low tonic pitch F in their answer. T. should stress the C-B-D middle area of the mode and ask students to do the same.

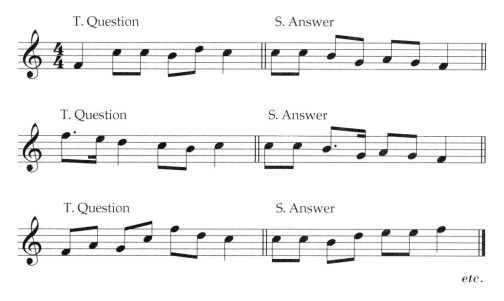

etc.

Make students aware of the repeated A phrase in the first section of the dance as part of an A-B-A-B1 structure. Teach them the A phrase in its simple form (melodic configuration #1 above) while T. answers the phrase with the B and B1 answers without the melodic extension (bars 5 & 6). S. can now add the embellishment to the A pattern. Eventually, switch roles with the students, having them focus on the descending scale pattern. Once secure, ask students to play the entire tune with the previously prepared accompaniment; they will need to hold the final note of the melody quite a while as the BX, AX and TB finish up the accompaniment. Students enjoy this challenge!

Develop the B section in the same manner; first exploring some isolated melodic patterns without rhythm, then playing them in rhythm in Q. and A. improvisations between student and teacher. Leave off the F pick-up notes to mm. 7–10 until the rest of the melody is secure, then add the pick-ups.

Students with advanced notation reading skills might benefit from reading the melody directly from the score but the teacher should keep in mind the steps noted above along with many others that allow an elementally-conceived melody to be broken down and taught without overly relying on the reading of notation.

Elemental music allows for many ways to perform the piece. Try adding Q. & A. improvisations into the performance. You might have students create text and sing the melody. The little coda (below) was created by a student in one of my classes.

Coda

11. A Bit of Orff

Steven Calantropio

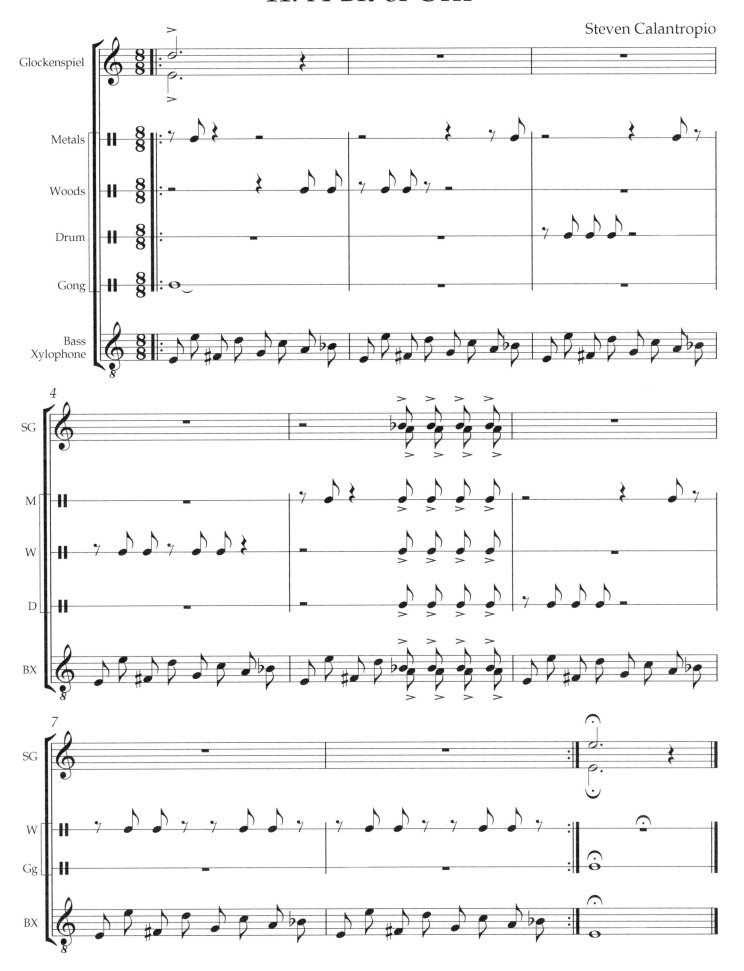

A Bit of Orff challenges modern students to explore the use of binary numerals as a foundation for music making. Since early times, numerical patterns have been used as the basis for musical invention in rhythm, melody, harmony and structure. As a reflection of our digital age, binary numerals using only two concepts of 1 and 0 (also interpreted as ON-black and OFF-white) are used to create a rhythmic pattern with a deeper meaning.

Exploration:

Using black and white index card stock, T. lays out a sample pattern of eight cards. Seven of the cards are white and one is black. It can be placed in any position (#1 below). While T. rhythmically counts the numerals "1, 2, 3 . . . 8" students must clap only the number where the black card is found. The pattern is repeated as an ostinato.

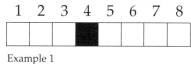

Example 1

Now T. uses two black cards in the eight card sequence (Example 2). The position of the black cards can also be performed in movement shapes, changing from one shape to the next on the articulated beats. Have students create various patterns using eight cards and perform them as ostinati using body percussion or movement shapes. Students can also explore the simultaneous performance of two contrasting patterns demonstrating the concept of complementary rhythms (Example 3)

1 2 3 4 5 6 7 8

Example 2

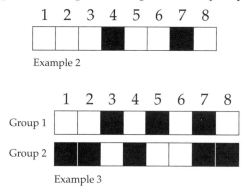

Example 3

Students will begin to realize that they are performing rhythms that have notational equivalents and that these rhythms have been converted to graphic representations. Visualizing these rhythms in 8/8 meter rather than 4/4 meter will help in understanding them.

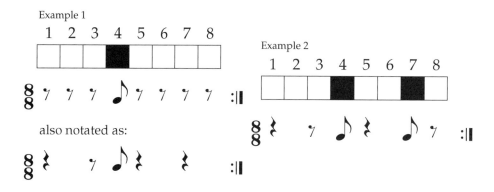

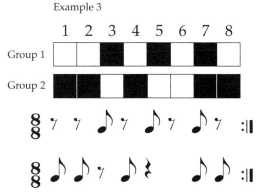

Example 3

In this system of graphic notation, quarter rest (𝄽) can substitute for any *two* consecutive empty boxes.

Next challenge students to understand the concept of binary numbers. suggest a sample number in traditional decimal counting such as 245. This is really three numbers with three different column values: the 2 in the hundreds column (200), the 4 in the tens column (40) and the 5 in the ones column (5). Adding these three columns together gives us the total 245 (below)

column value: 100 10 1

2	4	5

In binary counting only two symbols are used: 0 and 1. Each numeral is referred to as a binary digit (shortened to "bit"). The columns are not the powers of 10 as in decimal counting, but the powers of 2: an 8-column binary number known as a byte would have the following column organization:

128 64 32 16 8 4 2 1

A "1" in any column adds the value of that column to the total; a "0" in the column adds nothing. The decimal number 245 written in binary numerals would appear as follows:

128 64 32 16 8 4 2 1

1	1	1	1	0	1	0	1

expressed in decimal numbers as: 128 + 64 + 32 + 16 + 4 + 1 = 245

The conversion of decimal numbers into binary numbers will take some time for students (and teacher!) to gain facility with but is an important step in understanding digital information which is the foundation of much of our modern technology. Once the understanding of the use of ones and zeros to express numerical information is secure, it is an easy step to converting the numeral "1" to a black box and the numeral "0" to a white one:

128 64 32 16 8 4 2 1

= 245

Now another step is taken in viewing the eight columns of a binary number as the 8 eighth notes in a measure of 8/8 time. Our rhythms from the first part of this lesson can be interpreted as binary numbers and can be illustrated as:

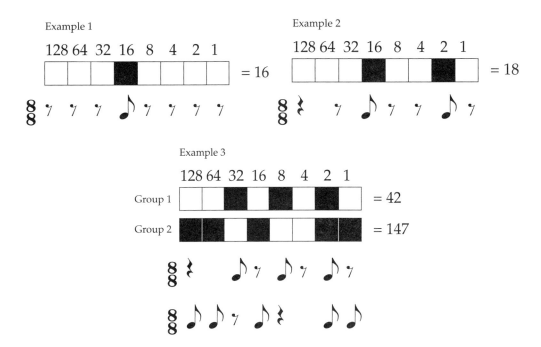

With some practice, students will become more adept at converting decimal numbers to binary numbers, converting binary numbers to 8/8 rhythms. This lesson is invaluable in linking music students to digital information by demonstrating how two contrasting parameters can convey numeric information (in this case, sound and silence).

Lesson Development
Prepare graphics of the eight binary numbers below and ask students to notate the musical rhythm for each in 8/8 time.

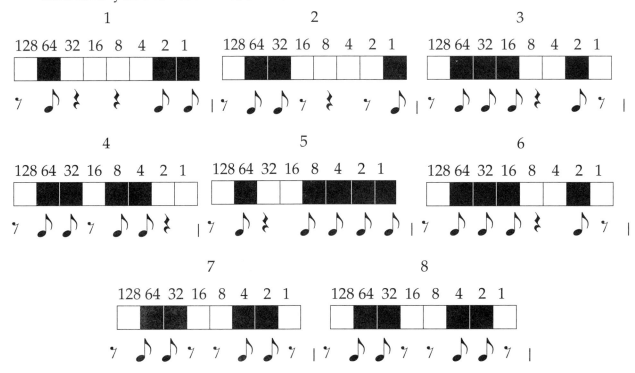

Counting such disjunct measures is made easier by adding an accompanying figure on the bass xylophone that plays all 8 eighth notes of each bar. The use of both F♯ and B♭ in the ostinato adds a chromatic feel to the pattern.

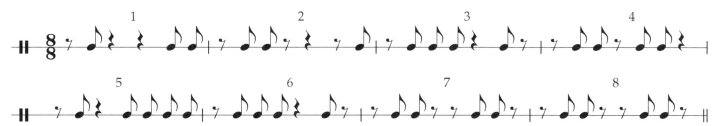

Have a student or students notate the eight rhythms sequentially on a blackboard. The class claps the resulting 8-bar rhythm accompanied by the BX ostinato pattern. Playing the BX pattern twice can serve as an introduction to this exercise.

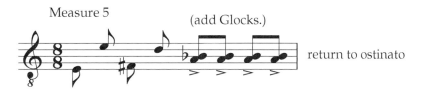

Ask students to look closely at the grouping of eighth notes in the entire pattern. A rest on both sides delineates a group. There are single notes, groups of two, groups of three and one group of four (in measure 5). Transfer the rhythm with accompaniment to body percussion sounds as follows:

♪ ____ = finger snap   ♪ ♪ ____ = two claps   ♪ ♪ ♪ = three knee pats

♪ ♪ ♪ ♪ ____ = pat, clap, snap, clap

Invite a player to lightly strike a large suspended gong with a triangle beater once at the start of the first measure. It will serve as a marker for when the complete rhythm begins. Have students repeat the rhythm twice, with the gong serving as the time marker on both repetitions. Add glockenspiels playing an octave E with the gong when it begins or repeats the pattern. Add a final E on BX and G. with a gong stroke after the second repetition has ended to mark the end of the exercise (see score).

Finally, transfer the single eighth note finger snap to small metal instruments (triangles, finger cymbals, agogo bell), the two eighth notes to wooden percussion (wood block, temple block, claves, etc.) and the three eighth note knee pats to various drums (hand drum, bongo, conga, djembe, etc.). Because the four eight note pattern happens only once in the fifth measure, it is articulated by all instruments. The BX breaks from its ostinato at that point and along with glockenspiels, plays the dissonant Bb/A pitches as scored (below).

Measure 5   (add Glocks.)

return to ostinato

While binary numbers may be interesting in themselves, the lesson takes a new direction with the introduction of ASCII code. ASCII stands for the American Standard Code for Information Interchange and is the common code used between computer platforms (MS-DOS, Mac OS, Linux, etc.) for exchanging information. 8-digit binary numbers are assigned to the characters of the keyboard; upper and lower case numbers, diacritical and expression markings, even an empty space. A partial listing of the ASCII code along with the decimal equivalent and character are shown.

Binary	Decimal	Character	Binary	Decimal	Character
01000001	65	A	01100001	97	a
01000010	66	B	01100010	98	b
01000011	67	C	01100011	99	c
01000100	68	D	01100100	100	d
01000101	69	E	01100101	101	e
01000110	70	F	01100110	102	f
01000111	71	G	01100111	103	g
01001000	72	H	01101000	104	h
01001001	73	I	01101001	105	i
01001010	74	J	01101010	106	j
01001011	75	K	01101011	107	k
01001100	76	L	01101100	108	l
01001101	77	M	01101101	109	m
01001110	78	N	01101110	110	n
01001111	79	O	01101111	111	o
01010000	80	P	01110000	112	p
01010001	81	Q	01110001	113	q
01010010	82	R	01110010	114	r
01010011	83	S	01110011	115	s
01010100	84	T	01110100	116	t
01010101	85	U	01110101	117	u
01010110	86	V	01110110	118	v
01010111	87	W	01110111	119	w
01011000	88	X	01111000	120	x
01011001	89	Y	01111001	121	y
01011010	90	Z	01111010	122	z

Ask students to decipher the decimal equivalent of each binary "measure" of music to discover the hidden meaning of this exercise.

Carl Orff developed a creative approach to music education known as Schulwerk that draws upon the natural musical instincts of all people. The Orff-Schulwerk is found in music classrooms all over the world.

Divergent Exercises
As an extension of this activity, challenge students to express other words in binary rhythms. Words with four or eight letters will work the best as they will better be felt as traditional musical phrases. Remember that any two opposite parameters can express a binary number (high-low, metal-wood, loud-soft, etc). Here are some possibilities:

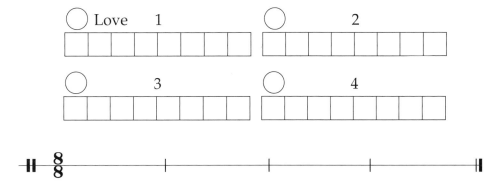

Challenge students to find the entire ASCII code including all diacritical and punctuation marks by entering the term "ASCII Code" in an internet search query.

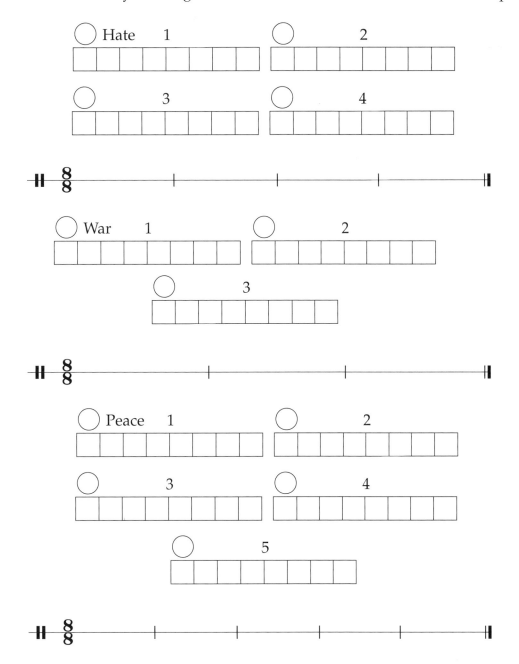

Digital information, expressed as two opposite parameters (black-white, on-off, accented-unaccented, one-zero, etc.) need not only convey numbers. They can be arranged to create a sort of rudimentary "drawing." The drawing can then be interpreted in sound or movement parameters.

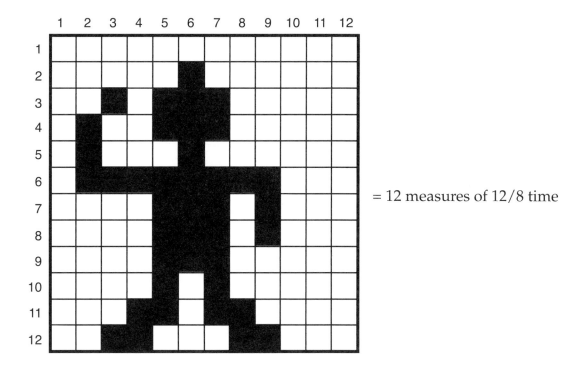

= 12 measures of 12/8 time

Such binary encoding of simple messages and "drawings" was one of the first ways that information from earth was beamed into space using radio wave transmission.

Pythagoras, the ancient Greek who codified some musical laws as early as 500 BC realized that music contained mathematical as well as geometrical patterns and although listeners were not consciously aware of these patterns, their presence affected the manner in which individuals responded to music

About the Author

Steven Calantropio spent 31 years teaching music and movement in the River Edge New Jersey public school system. Certified in Orff-Schulwerk since 1979, he also has studied the methodologies of Zoltan Kodály and Emile Jaques-Dalcroze. Mr. Calantropio received his BS from William Paterson University and his MFA from Ohio University. He has taught at numerous workshops, conferences and courses both nationally and internationally. Passionate about the possibilities of elemental music and movement to enrich people's lives, he is President and a founding member of the American Center for Elemental Music and Movement (ACEMM). Steve lives in New Jersey's scenic northern highlands region in the small town of Hamburg

Orff-Schulwerk American Edition

MAIN VOLUMES

Music for Children 1	Pre-School	SMC 12
Music for Children 2	Primary	SMC 6
Music for Children 3	Upper Elementary	SMC 8

SUPPLEMENTARY PUBLICATIONS

AFRICAN SONGS FOR SCHOOL AND COMMUNITY
(Robert Kwami)   SMC 551
A selection of 12 songs including traditional material and original compositions by the author.

THE ANCIENT FACE OF NIGHT (Gerald Dyck)   SMC 553
A collection of original songs and instrumental pieces for SATB chorus and Orff instruments. The cycle of songs has both astronomical and musical influences. (Chorus Part: SMC 553-01)

ANIMAL CRACKER SUITE AND OTHER POEMS
(Deborah A. Imiolo-Schriver)   SMC 561
A set of four original poems arranged for speech chorus, body percussion and percussion ensemble. Twenty-one additional original poems are included for teachers and students to make their own musical settings.

ALL AROUND THE BUTTERCUP (Ruth Boshkoff)   SMC 24
These folk-song arrangements are organized progressively, each new note being introduced separately.

CHIPMUNKS, CICADAS AND OWLS (Natalie Sarrazin)   SMC 552
Twelve native American children's songs from different regions.

CIRCUS RONDO (Donald Slagel)   SMC 73
A stylized circus presentation using music, movement, speech and improvisational technique, for various Orff instruments, recorders and voices.

CROCODILE AND OTHER POEMS (Ruth Pollock Hamm)   SMC 15
A collection of verses for use as choral speech within the elementary school. Included are ideas for movement, instrumental accompaniments, and proposals for related art, drama and listening activities.

DANCING SONGS (Phillip Rhodes)   SMC 35
A song cycle for voices and Orff instruments. The contemporary harmonies create a dramatic and sophisticated experience for upper elementary/middle school grades.

DE COLORES (Virginia Ebinger)   SMC 20
Folklore from the Hispanic tradition for voices, recorders and classroom percussion.

DISCOVERING KEETMAN (Jane Frazee)   SMC 547
Rhythmic exercises and pieces for xylophone by Gunild Keetman. Selected and introduced by Jane Frazee.

DOCUM DAY (Donald Slagel)   SMC 18
An olio of songs from England, Hungary, Ireland, Jamaica, the Middle East, Newfoundland, Nova Scotia, the USA. For voices, recorders and classroom percussion.

EIGHT MINIATURES (Hermann Regner)   SMC 14
Ensemble pieces for advanced players of recorders and Orff instruments which lead directly from elementary "Music for Children" to chamber music for recorders.

ELEMENTAL RECORDER PLAYING
(Gunild Keetman and Minna Ronnefeld) Translation by Mary Shamrock
Teacher's Book   SMC 558
Based on the fundamental principles of Orff-Schulwerk, this book can be used as a foundation text in an elementary music program that includes use of the recorder. It can also be employed in teaching situations that concentrate primarily upon recorder but in which ensemble playing, improvisation and singing also play an essential role.
Student's Book   SMC 559
Includes a variety of songs, pieces, improvisation exercises, canons, duets, rondos and texts to use for making rhythms and melodies.
Student's Workbook   SMC 560
Contains exercises and games for doing at home and during the music lesson. Integrated with work in the Student's Book.

FENCE POSTS AND OTHER POEMS (Ruth Pollock Hamm)   SMC 31
Texts for melodies, "Sound Envelopes," movement and composition written by children, selected poets and the editor. Material for creative melody making and improvisation (including jazz).

FOUR PSALM SETTINGS (Sue Ellen Page)   SMC 30
For treble voices (unison and two-part) and Orff instruments.

HAVE YOU ANY WOOL? THREE BAGS FULL! (Richard Gill)   SMC 29
17 traditional rhymes for voices and Orff instruments. Speech exercises, elaborate settings for Orff instruments using nursery rhymes to show how to play with texts.

HELLO CHILDREN (Shirley Salmon)   SMC 572
A collection of songs and related activities for children aged 4–9

I'VE GOT A SONG IN BALTIMORE   SMC574
Folk-songs of North America and the British Isles

KUKURÍKU (Miriam Samuelson)   SMC 57
Traditional Hebrew songs and dances (including Hava Nagila) arranged for voices, recorders and Orff instruments. Instructions (with diagrams) are given for the dances.

THE MAGIC FOREST (Lynn Johnson)   SMC 16
Sequenced, early childhood, music-lesson plans based on the Orff-Schulwerk approach.

PIECES AND PROCESSES (Steven Calantropio)   SMC 569
This collection of original songs, exercises, instrumental pieces, and arrangements provides fresh examples of elemental music. Along with each piece is a detailed teaching procedure designed to give music educators a collection of instructional techniques.

THE QUANGLE WANGLE'S HAT (Sara Newberry)   SMC 32
Edward Lear's delightful poem set for speaker(s), recorders and Orff instruments (with movement and dance improvisation).

¡QUIEN CANTA SU MAL ESPANTA!
Songs, Games and Dances from Latin America
(Sofia Lopez-Ibor and Verena Maschat)   SMC 568
This book presents a rich and varied selection of material from an immense geographical area, combining local traditions with foreign influences to engage and inspire teachers and students. The DVD includes demonstrations of the dances for presentation in the classroom.

THE RACCOON PHILOSOPHER
(Danai Gagne-Apostolidou and Judith Thomas-Solomon)   SMC 566
A drama in mixed meters for upper elementary grades with preparatory activities for singing, moving, playing recorder, Orff instruments and creating. The Raccoon Philosopher was inspired by thoughts on virtue by Martin Buber. As we learn from the raccoon, so we learn from the children: to be merry for no particular reason, to never for a moment be idle, and to express our needs vigorously.

RECORDERS WITH ORFF ENSEMBLE (Isabel McNeill Carley) SMC 25-27
Three books designed to fill a need for a repertoire (pentatonic and diatonic) for beginning and intermediate recorder players. Most of the pieces are intended to be both played and danced and simple accompaniments are provided.

RINGAROUND, SINGAROUND (Ruth Boshkoff)   SMC 33
Games, rhymes and folk-songs for the early elementary grades, arranged in sequential order according to concepts.

ROUND THE CORNER AND AWAY WE GO (David J. Gonzol)   SMC 567
This folk-song collection provides models of arrangements to be taught using Orff-Schulwerk processes. The accompanying teaching suggestions give examples of how to break down instrumental parts and sequence the presentation of them developmentally.

RRRRRO
(Polyxene Mathéy and Angelika Panagopoulos-Slavik)   SMC 79
Poetry, music and dance from Greece with Greek texts adapted for rhythmic reciting by groups accompanied by percussion and other instruments.

A SEASONAL KALEIDOSCOPE
(Joyce Coffey, Danai Gagne, Laura Koulish)   SMC 55
Original songs, poetry and stories with Orff instruments for children. Bound by a theme of seasonal changes and intended for classroom and music teachers.

SHALOM CHAVEIRIM
(Robert A. Amchin)   SMC 575
A celebration of Jewish and Hebrew music for voices and Orff Ensemble

SIMPLY SUNG (Mary Goetze)   SMC 23
Folk-songs arranged in three parts for young singers. They include American folk-songs, spirituals and Hebrew melodies.

SKETCHES IN STYLE (Carol Richards and Neil Aubrey)   SMC 19
Arrangements for classroom music. For voices, recorders and classroom percussion.

SOMETHING TOLD THE WILD GEESE (Craig Earley)   SMC 21
A collection of folk songs for unison treble voices, barred and small percussion instruments, and recorders (soprano and alto).

STREET GAMES (Gloria Fuoco-Lawson)   SMC 17
Instrumental arrangements of rhythmical hand jives based on traditional American street games.

TALES TO TELL, TALES TO PLAY
(Carol Erion and Linda Monssen)   SMC 28
Four folk tales (Indian, African, German and American Indian) retold and arranged for music and movement, with accompaniment for recorders and Orff instruments.

TEN FOLK CAROLS FOR CHRISTMAS FROM THE UNITED STATES
(Jane Frazee)   SMC 22
Settings of Appalachian and unfamiliar carols, arranged for voices, recorders and Orff instruments.

TUNES FOR YOUNG TROUBADOURS (Dianne Ladendecker)   SMC 34
Ten songs for children's voices, recorders and Orff ensemble.

WIND SONGS (Phillip Rhodes)   SMC 197
Four songs for unison voices, barred and small percussion instruments.